Prescription: Laughter

The Kennedy Wit

The Stevenson Wit

The Churchill Wit

Presidential Wit—From Washington to Johnson

The Washington Wits

Letters from Camp

Kids' Letters to President Kennedy

Dear President Johnson

Dear Senator Kennedy

Letters to the Air Force on UFOs

Kids' Letters to the FBI

Letters from Vietnam

Dear Internal Revenue

Funniest Fan Letters to Batman

Dear Smokey Bear

Dear 007

Love Letters to the Beatles

Love Letters to the Mets

Boys Are Very Funny People

The Common Sense Wisdom of Three First Ladies

John F. Kennedy and the Young People of America

Pope Paul in the United States

The Pope John Album

PRESCRIPTION: LAUGHTER

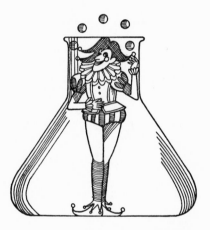

An Anthology of Medical Merriment

EDITED BY WILLIAM ADLER

Illustrations by Loring Eutemey

HARCOURT, BRACE & WORLD, INC., NEW YORK

"Aesculapius and the Early Greeks" and "Hippocrates and the Later Greeks" are from *It All Started with Hippocrates,* by Richard Armour, copyright © 1966 by Richard Armour, used by permission of the McGraw-Hill Book Company. "Say the Case Is Grave" is from *Call the Doctor,* by E. S. Turner, © 1958 by E. S. Turner, reprinted by permission of St. Martin's Press, Inc., and Michael Joseph, London. "Sawbones' Apprentice, Getting Acquainted with the Medicines" is from *Louisiana Swamp Doctor: The Life and Writings of Henry Clay Lewis,* edited by John Q. Anderson, copyright © 1962 by Louisiana State University Press, reprinted by permission of Louisiana State University Press. "Preface on Doctors" is from *The Doctor's Dilemma,* by George Bernard Shaw, reprinted by permission of the Public Trustee and the Society of Authors. "The Soldier Who Saw Everything Twice" is from *Catch–22,* by Joseph Heller, copyright © 1955, 1961 by Joseph Heller, reprinted by permission of Simon & Schuster, Inc. "An Ordeal to Choke a Sword-Swallower," by Shana Alexander, is from *Life* Magazine, January 21, 1966, © 1966 Time Inc., all rights reserved. "Silver Lining," by R. G. G. Price, is copyright © 1966 by The Atlantic Monthly Company, Boston, Mass., 02116, reprinted with permission. "Is It Fatal, Doc?" is from *The Love Everybody Crusade,* by Arthur Hoppe, copyright © 1963 by Arthur Hoppe, reprinted by permission of Doubleday & Company, Inc. "The Miracle Drugs Abroad" is from *Don't Forget to Write,* by Art Buchwald, copyright © 1958, 1959, 1960 by Art Buchwald, reprinted by permission of The World Publishing Company. "Operation Frame-up" is from *The Medical Itch* by Claude Benjamin, copyright © 1964 by Claude Benjamin, reprinted by permission of Ivan Obolensky, Inc. "Did I Ever Tell You About My Operation?" is from *And How Do We Feel This Morning?,* by Corey Ford, illustrated by Eric Gurney, © 1964 by Eric Gurney, published by Prentice-Hall, Inc., Englewood Cliffs, New Jersey. "Operation Operation" is from *Please Don't Eat the Daisies,* by Jean Kerr, copyright © 1957 by Jean Kerr,

I would like to thank my fine staff—David Curtis, Elaine Crane, Catherine Johnston, and Janice Van Raay—for their able assistance in the preparation of this book.

Foreword

Medical humor is undoubtedly as old as the practice of medicine itself, if not older. It has been suggested, in fact, that the first doctor joke was the first doctor bill. At any rate, the essential relationship of doctor and patient endures unchanged by time or custom:

> The physician said, "Sir, you are an old man." "That happens," replied Pausanias, "because you were never my doctor."

The humor in this jibe, recorded over eighteen hundred years ago by Plutarch, is as cogent for today's reader as it was for the first-century Greek.

There are some skeptics who insist that medical practices have not advanced very much either. "After all," they point out, "even our Anglo-Saxon forefathers called their physicians 'leeches.'" But such cynics are in the minority. Few will deny that medical techniques have improved immeasurably over those of times past, when a doctor's treatment could quite literally have cost "an arm and a leg." Happily, the sharpness of the doctor's wit has kept pace with that of his scalpel.

This book is dedicated to inducing laughter, the only form of contagion that doctors dare regard as a blessing. To further the spread of this contagion, I have collected choice samples of infectious medical humor in its most virulent forms. The book includes selections

by such well-known outpatients as George Bernard
Shaw, Robert Benchley, Cornelia Otis Skinner, S. J.
Perelman, Art Buchwald, Jean Kerr, Richard Armour,
Goodman Ace, and Joseph Heller.

The whole hilarious gamut of the medical world is
covered from the familiar agony of the dentist's chair
to the ecstasy of the "blessed event," and includes
mirthful excursions into medicine's not-too-distant past.
So if you're in good health, consider yourself fortunate,
and by all means have a few chuckles on me. If you're
a hypochondriac you will find a wealth of new ideas for
diseases that may exceed your wildest fantasies—in addition to the satisfaction of knowing that your affliction
places you in the company of Goodman Ace, *et al.* If
you're sick, please get well soon, and meanwhile take
a dose or two of laughter, truly the best tonic.

William Adler
New York City

Contents

Prescription: Laughter

CHAPTER I

Medical History
Revisited

The path taken by medicine to reach its present-day status has hardly been straight and narrow. Like most fields of learning in the Western World, it got off to a fairly good start with the Greeks and Romans, but bogged down considerably in the Dark and Middle Ages. Then came the Renaissance, and with it the vital infusions of humanism and enlightenment which led to the breakthroughs that liberated medicine from the shackles of ignorance and superstition.

It all sounds deadly serious, but, as Richard Armour and his fellow medical chroniclers demonstrate, getting here was lots of fun. Whatever else these writers have been liberated from, they have certainly retained their senses of humor. With them we revisit the history of medicine, starting with Aesculapius, continuing through the days of Chaucerian England, and including a taste of medicine as it was "practiced" in World War II. It's a whirlwind tour spanning three continents and two millennia, and it may leave you a little dizzy or weak with laughter. But it will also offer you a brand-new perspective on modern medicine.

Aesculapius and the Early Greeks

RICHARD ARMOUR

Babylonia and Egypt, we are told, "handed the torch of medical learning to the Greeks." Those who are familiar with the opening ceremony of the Olympic Games will be able to visualize this: a Babylonian doctor, with a torch held in his outstretched hand, running until he comes to another doctor who takes the torch and runs to another doctor who takes the torch and runs to another doctor, until at last the final doctor, torch in hand, staggers across the Greek border. The doctor is carried to the nearest hospital, suffering from exhaustion, dehydration, and third-degree burns on the arms and face, while the torch is used on a patient who had been waiting all this time to have a running sore[1] cauterized.

The Greeks gave a good deal of credit for medical advances to Apollo, the god of health, whose temple was at Delphi. People came from all over Greece for help. Apollo was not there himself, but he worked through an answering service. This was a priestess[2] who sat, chewing laurel leaves, by a cleft in the rock out of which came intoxicating fumes. People would tell her their symptoms and she would chew thought-

1. Not to be confused with a running doctor.
2. Or Sibyl, who hissed slightly, speaking in sibylants.

fully a few times, breathe deeply of the fumes, and give a prognosis. Actually the information came from Apollo, who was at the other end of the fumes, within easy reach of his Materia Medica.

Apollo taught the healing art to Chiron, a centaur who later became the god of surgery, and Chiron in turn taught Aesculapius. Since Chiron was half horse and half man, he was none too easy to teach, restlessly twitching his tail and often galloping off before the lesson was over, having spied an attractive filly.

As for Aesculapius, he was Apollo's son by an earth-maiden, Coronis. According to Hesiod, Apollo one day surprised Coronis bathing. She was not only surprised but astonished that Apollo, a god, would look at her, a little old virgin, that way. Anyhow, she tried to cover her embarrassment, being unable to cover anything else, and soon was carrying Apollo's child.[1] Unfortunately, her father had promised her to her cousin Ischus, and her condition was, after a few months, pretty obvious. To make a long story short, Apollo shot Ischus with an arrow, Artemis did likewise to Coronis, and then Apollo, feeling sorry for Coronis on her funeral pyre, snatched his unborn son, Aesculapius, from his mother's womb in what was surely the first instance of a Caesarean section.

Eventually Aesculapius took over Apollo's practice at Delphi, performing many miraculous cures, helped by his daughters Hygeia and Panacea, not to mention Edema and Pyorrhea. He was also helped by a trained

1. And not in her arms.

snake, or medical technician, who went along to do little things such as licking a patient's sores or, if the patient could hold still, his eyelids.[1]

As Aesculapius' name became known, he opened branches, known as Asklepieia, all over Greece. It was not ethical to advertise. Nor, as a matter of fact, was it necessary. His fame traveled to the remote coroners of Greece, and the sick hastened to the nearest Asklepieion for Aesculapius' patented cure. This was known as "incubation," or temple-sleep. The patient came to the temple (or incubator), went to sleep, and had a dream in which Aesculapius appeared and performed the treatment. After an incubation period of about eight hours, the patient awakened, feeling fine. It was a foolproof method, everyone being cured except an occasional insomniac.[2]

One of Aesculapius' more spectacular cures, not widely achieved by physicians even today, was restoring the dead to life. What with curing his own patients and bringing back to life the patients of less successful doctors, Aesculapius was riding high. Then Pluto, the ruler of the Underworld, began to fear a shortage of population in his realm. So he appealed to Zeus,[3] who accommodatingly slew Aesculapius with a thunderbolt.

But don't feel sorry for Aesculapius. He was pro-

1. If you have never had your eyelids licked by a snake, and are not ticklish, try it. Some find it as relaxing as a foot rub by a podiatrist.

2. Sometimes, instead of curing the patient while he slept, Aesculapius merely gave him a diagnosis, leaving treatment to his personal physician (priest) as a matter of professional courtesy.

3. Pluto appealed to very few.

moted from a demigod to a god, and lived happily ever after.[1]

                                FROM *It All Started with Hippocrates*

Hippocrates and the Later Greeks
RICHARD ARMOUR

Before Hippocrates, medicine was in the hands of priests.[2] The priests thought diseases were caused by demons and angry gods, which still sounds pretty plausible. But Hippocrates thought sickness could be traced to natural causes, such as bad diet, lack of fresh air, too much carousing around, and falling off the top of the Parthenon.

"In truth we know little or nothing of Hippocrates," says one historian, preparatory to writing of him at length. It seems Hippocrates was born in 460 B.C., which, if our subtraction is correct, made him 105 years old at the time of his death. His ability to keep himself alive so long must have been one reason he gained the confidence of his patients.[3]

But if Hippocrates lived a long time, think of the large plane tree, still pointed out as the one under whose shade he once taught his pupils. The age of this

1. As for his snake, it wound up (or around) a staff or wand, known as a caduceus.

2. In other words D.D.'s, not M.D.'s.

3. A doctor suffering from a miserable head cold is always looked at a little skeptically when he holds out a handful of pills and says, "Take one of these three times a day and you'll feel better."

tree is estimated at around 2500 years, which shows that it knows a few things about health unknown to Hippocrates. But then, it stays out in the fresh air more than Hippocrates did, though it gets less exercise.

Hippocrates was born on the island of Cos, which explains the title of one of his many treatises, *The Cos and Effect of Disease*. Legend has it that he was once a librarian and was forced to flee when he burned some old medical books. Why he burned these books is not known. Did they disagree with his theories? An overworked librarian, was he tired of putting them back on the right shelf when they were misplaced by careless medical students? Was he cold, and out of kindling? The reader is left to his own conjectures.

Whether or not Hippocrates was forced to flee because of something he did as a librarian, there seems no doubt that he was an itinerant doctor. Since he had no office and for some reason declined to make house calls, he had to treat patients wherever he found them—on the streets,[1] in the groves of Academe, or in the public bath. The bath was perhaps the most convenient, because patients wishing a thorough examination were already disrobed and ready to go. Anyhow, Hippocrates kept on the move, looking for a good plague. As Hippocrates' reputation grew, people came to him from all over Greece. This was flattering to Hippocrates but not to the patient's own doctor.

"What's this Hippocrates got that I haven't got?" the family physician would ask, with just a trace of a sneer. But there was no reply, because his former patients were too busy packing to go look for Hippocrates.

1. Accident victims.

There was a report he was last seen in Macedonia. Or was it Thrace? With Hippocrates wandering around looking for patients and patients wandering around looking for Hippocrates, there was a good deal of confusion.

Hippocrates based his medical practice on observation and reasoning, which have been the foundation of medicine ever since. For example, he would ask a patient to stick out his tongue, and he would look at it (observation). If it had a layer of whitish stuff on it, he would say to himself, "Aha, he had vanilla ice cream for dessert!" (reasoning). He was less interested in treatment than in diagnosis. Once he had figured out what was the matter with a patient and had told him, he felt he had discharged his responsibility. From then on, the patient could do the worrying. He was the one who was sick, wasn't he? [1]

An example of Hippocrates' method of practice was the time the King of Macedonia fell sick and his doctors thought he had phthisis[2]—he was off his rocker. Did Hippocrates attempt to cure the King? Did he tell the King, "Sire, you are nuts?" No, Hippocrates, who not only knew how to diagnose but when to keep his mouth shut, headed back to Athens as fast as he could go. Hippocrates has been called the Ideal Physician, and no wonder.

There are some fascinating legends about Hippoc-

1. Hippocrates believed it was up to nature to do the healing. He referred his patients to nature the way G.P.'s today refer their patients to specialists.
2. If you have trouble pronouncing "phthisis," you might be interested to know that one of Hippocrates' biographers was named Tzetzes.

rates. One is that he never gave a thought to money. Another is that he admitted his errors. The reader should keep in mind that these are legends.

Ever since Hippocrates, graduating medical students take the Hippocratic oath, which starts out, "I swear." After they have been in practice a few years they learn how right Hippocrates was, and how much there is to swear about

FROM *It All Started with Hippocrates*

Say the Case Is Grave

E. S. TURNER

The doctors of Chaucer's day inherited from the ancient world the rules of their profession as well as the bulk of their medical knowledge. They had, however, a more practical, workaday code in which the austere Greek ideals, as defined in the Hippocratic Oath, were relieved by a dash or two of cynicism and self-interest.

Some of these worldlier notions were gathered at Salerno, where medicine was privileged to flourish in the Dark Ages (Ages so Dark that even women were trained to become doctors). The early English writers on medicine sometimes passed off these maxims as their own, with pious or sardonic additions. It would be tedious to try to unscramble the sources, to trace such-and-such a piece of advice to Hippocrates or Galen, and such-and-such to Archimathaeus or Arnold of Villianova. The most convenient, if not the most scholarly, course is to summarise the code and to say that it represents, in part if not in whole, the views of men like John of Gaddesden, the first Englishman to hold the appointment of Court physician; John of Mirfield, who laboured in the priory of St. Bartholomew, in London; and John of Arderne, the first outstanding English surgeon.

The rules are as follows:

Dress soberly like a clerk, not like a minstrel. Keep your finger nails well shaped and clean.

Do not walk hastily, which betokens levity, or too slowly, which is a sign of faint-heartedness.

When called to a patient, find out from his messenger as much about him as you can before you arrive. Then, if his pulse and urine tell you nothing, you can still surprise him with your knowledge of his condition.

On arrival, exchange greetings, accept refreshment in the spirit in which it is offered, remark on the beauty of the countryside and of the house, and praise the liberality of the family (but only if such compliments seem merited).

Whenever possible, ensure that the patient has confessed before you examine him. If you wait until after your examination before advising him to confess, he will suspect the worst.

When feeling the patient's pulse, allow for the fact that he may be disturbed by your arrival and by the thought of the fee you are going to charge him.

Do not be in a hurry to give an opinion on the patient. It will be more valued by the family if they have to wait for it.

Hide your instruments from the sight of the patient—and from other doctors.

Tell the patient that, with God's help, you hope to cure him, but inform the relatives that the case is grave. Then, if he dies, you will have safeguarded yourself. If he recovers, it will be a testimony to your skill and wisdom. When asked how long recovery will take, specify double the expected period. A quicker recovery will redound to your credit, whereas if a patient finds the cure taking longer than prophesied, he will lose faith in your skill. If he asks why the cure was so swift, tell him he was strong-hearted and had good healing flesh; he will then be proud and delighted.

Behave modestly and gravely at all times.

Do not sow dissension among the servants or offer them unsolicited advice, or brawl with anybody in the house.

Do not look lecherously on the patient's wife, daughters or maid-servants, or kiss them, or fondle their breasts (an affable old medieval custom) or whisper to them in corners. Such conduct distracts the physician's mind from his work and is likely to draw on the house the wrath of God, who is watching over the patient. It may also disturb the patient and fill him with suspicions and worries which will negative any good that may be wrought by the medicine.

If you are asked to dinner, do not be over-effusive in your gratitude, and do not quibble about accepting the place of honour at the table. Be neither indiscreet nor exacting. Do not criticise the food, even if it is millet bread which turns your stomach. Stay sober. During the meal, enquire frequently after the patient, lest he suspect that you have forgotten him in your enjoyment of his viands.

Do not talk boastfully, especially among great men, lest they trip you up in your own words.

Do not disparage your fellow physicians. If you do not know them personally, say you have heard nothing but good of them.

Avoid the company or friendship of laymen. They make a habit of mocking doctors, and besides, it is not always easy to extract a fee from an intimate.

Tell the patient funny stories as well as recommending him to serious contemplations and to the Scriptures.

If you do not wish to take on a case, pretend to be ill.

If you find the patient dead on your arrival, show no surprise. Say you knew from the account of his symptoms he would not recover and enquire the hour at which he died. This will enhance your professional reputation.

FROM *Call the Doctor*

Directions, for recovering persons, who are supposed to be dead, from drowning.

Published at the behest of the Humane Society of Philadelphia in the July 7, 1787 New York Daily Advertiser, this advice reveals much about the state of eighteenth-century medicine.

1st. As soon as the body is taken out of the water it must be conveyed, *with care and tenderness,* to a house, or any other place, where it can be laid dry and warm, avoiding the usual destructive methods of *hanging it by the heels, rolling it on a barrel, or placing it across a log, on the belly.*

2dly. The cloaths must be immediately stripped off, and the body wrapped up in blankets, well warmed. It should be laid on its back, with the head a little raised. If the weather be cold, it should be placed near a fire; but if the weather should be warm, it will be sufficient to place it between two blankets well heated; taking care to prevent the room from being crowded with any persons who are not necessarily employed about the body.

3dly. As soon as it can possibly be done, a bellows should be applied to one nostril, while the other nostril and the mouth are kept closed, and the lower end of the prominent part of the wind-pipe (or that part which is called by anatomists *pontum Adami*) is pressed backward. The bellows is to be worked in this situation; and when the breast is swelled by it, the bellows should stop, and an assistant should press the belly upwards, to force the air out. The bellows should then be applied as before, and the belly should again be pressed upwards; and this process should be repeated from 20 to 30 times in a minute, so as to imitate natural breathing as nearly as possible. Some volatile spirits, heated, should be held under the valve of the bellows, while it works. If a bellows cannot be procured, some person should blow into one of the nostrils through a pipe or quill, while the other nostril and mouth are closed as before; or if a pipe or quill be not at hand, he should blow into the mouth, while both nostrils are closed; but whenever a bellows can be procured, it should be preferred, as air forced in by this means will be much more serviceable than air which has been already breathed.

4thly. At the same time, the whole body should be rubbed with the hand, or with hot woollen cloths. The rubbing should be moderate, but continued with industry a long time, and particularly about the breast.

5thly. During this time, a large quantity of ashes, or salt, or sand, should be heated; and as soon as it is milk-warm, the body should be placed in it; the blowing and rubbing are then to be continued as before; and when the ashes, salt or sand, are cooled, some warmer must be added, so that the whole may be kept milk-warm.

These methods should be continued three or four hours, as in several instances they have proved successful, altho' no signs of life appeared until that time. When the patient is able to swallow, he should take some wine, or rum and water; bleeding or purging ought not to be used without consulting a physician, who should be called in as soon as possible.

Sawbones' Apprentice,
Getting Acquainted with the Medicines

HENRY CLAY LEWIS

"Now, Mr. Tensas," said my kind preceptor, a few days after I had got regularly installed in the office, "your first duty must be to get acquainted with the different medicines. This is a Dispensatory—as you read of a drug you will find the majority mentioned on the shelves, take it down and digest"—here, unfortunately for the peace of mind and general welfare of a loafing Indian, who hung continually around the office seeking what he might devour, or rather steal, the doctor was called away in a great hurry and did not have time to finish his sentence. "Take it down and digest" were the last words that remained in my mind. "Take it down and digest." By the father of physic, thought I, this study of medicine is not the pleasant task I anticipated —rather arduous in the long run for the stomach, I should judge, to swallow and digest all the medicines from Abracadabra to Zanzibar. Why, some of them are vomits, and I'd like to know how they are to be kept down long enough to be digested. Now, as for tamarinds, or liquorice, or white sugar, I might go them, but aloes, and rhubarb, and castor oil, and running your finger down your throat are rather disagreeable any way you can take them. I'm in for it, though; I suppose it's the way all doctors are made, and I have no claims to be exempted; and now for the big book with the long name.

I opened it upon a list of the metals. Leading them in the order that alphabetical arrangement entitled it to, was "Arsenic: *deadly poison*. Best preparation, Fowler's Solution, Symptoms from an overdose, burning in the stomach, great thirst, excessive vomiting," etc., etc. With eyes distended to their utmost capacity, I read the dread enumeration of its properties. What! take this infernal medicament down, digest it, and run the chances of its not being an overdose? Can't think of it a moment. I'll go back to my plough first; but then the doctor knew all the dangers when he gave his directions, and he was so precise and particular that there cannot be any mistake. I'll take a look at it anyhow, and I hunted it up. As the Dispensatory preferred Fowler's Solution, I selected that. Expecting to find but a small quantity, I was somewhat surprised when I discovered it in a four-gallon bottle, nearly full. I took out the stopper and applied it cautiously to my nose. Had it not been for the label bearing in addition to the name the fearful word "Poison" and the ominous skull and crossbones, I would have sworn it was good old Bourbon whiskey. Old Tubba, the Indian, was sitting in the office door, watching my proceedings with a great deal of interest. Catching the spirituous odor of the arsenical solution, he rose up and approached me eagerly, saying, "Ugh," Injun want whiskey: give Tubba whiskey; bring wild duck, so many," holding up two of his fingers. The temptation was strong, I must confess. The medicines had to be tested, and I felt very much disinclined to depart this life just

then, when the pinfeathers of science had just com-
menced displacing the soft down of ducklingdom; but
this Indian, he is of no earthly account or use to any
one; no one would miss him, even were he to take an
overdose; science often has demanded sacrifices, and he
would be a willing one; but—it may kill him; I can't do
it; to kill a man before I get my diploma will be murder;
a jury might not so pronounce it, but conscience would;
I can't swallow it, and Tubba must not. These were the
thoughts that flashed through my mind before I replied
to the Indian's request. "Indian can't have whiskey.
Tubba drink whiskey—Tubba do so." Here I endeav-
ored to go through the pantomime of dying, as I was
not master of sufficient Choctaw to explain myself. I
lifted a glass to my mouth and pretended to empty it,
then gave a short yell, clapping my hands over my
stomach, staggering, jerking my hands and feet about,
as I fell on the floor, repeating the yells, then turned on
my face and lay still as though I were dead. But to my
chagrin, all this did not seem to affect the Indian with
that horror that I intended, but on the contrary, he
grunted out a series of ughs, expressive of his satisfaction, saying, "Ugh, Tubba want get drunk too."

The dinner hour arriving, I dismissed old Tubba, and
arranging my toilet, walked up to the dwelling house,
near half a mile distant, where I was detained several
hours by the presence of company, to whom I was
forced to do the honors, the doctor not having returned.

At length I got released and returned to the office,
resolving to suspend my studies until I could have a
talk with my preceptor; for, even on my ignorant mind,
the shadow of a doubt was falling as to whether there

might not be some mistake in my understanding of his
language.

As I entered the office, my eyes involuntarily sought
the Solution of Arsenic. Father of purges and pukes, it
was gone! "Tubba, you're a gone case. I ought to have
hidden it. I might have known he would steal it after
smelling the whiskey; poor fellow! it's no use to try and
find him, he's struck a straight line for the swamp;
poor fellow! it's all my fault." Thus upbraiding myself
for my carelessness, I walked back into my bedroom.
And my astonishment may be imagined, when I discovered the filthy Indian tucked in nicely between my
clean sheets.

To all appearances he was in a desperate condition,
the fatal bottle lying hugged closely in his embrace,
nearly empty. He must be suffering awfully, thought I,
when humanity had triumphed over the indignation I
felt at the liberties he had taken, but Indian-like, he
bears it without a groan. Well has his race been called
"the stoics of the wood, the men without a tear." But
I must not let him die without an effort to save him. I
don't know what to do myself, so I'll call in Dr. B., and
away I posted; but Dr. B. was absent; so was Dr. L., and
in fact every physician of the town. Each office, however, contained one or more students; and as half a loaf
is better than no bread, I speedily informed them of the
condition of affairs, and quickly, like a flock of young
vultures, we were thronging around the poisoned Indian, to whom we would soon have rendered the harvest of death.

"Stomach pump eo instanti!" said one; "Sulphas Zinci
cum Decoction Tabacum!" said another; "Venesection!"

suggested a third. "Puke of Lobelia!" suggested a young
disciple of Thompson, who self-invited had joined the
conclave. "Lobelia. Number six, pepper tea, yaller pow-
ders, I say!" "Turn him out! Turn him out! What rights
has young Roots in a mineral consultation? Turn him
out!"—and heels over head, out of the room, through
the middle door, and down the office steps, went
"young Roots," impelled by the whole body of the enraged "regulars"—save myself, who, determined amidst
the array of medical lore not to appear ignorant, wisely
held my tongue and rubbed the patient's feet with a
greased rag. Again rose the jargon of voices.

"Sulphas Zinci—Stomach, Arteri, pump, otomy—
must—legs—hot toddy—to bleed him—lectricity—hot
blister—flatirons—open his—windpipe"; but still I said
never a word, but rubbed his feet, wondering whether
I would ever acquire as much knowledge as my fellow
students showed the possession of. By the bye, I was
the only one that was doing anything for the patient,
the others being too busy discussing the case to attend
to the administration of any one of the remedies pro-
posed.

"I say stimulate, the system is sinking," screamed a
tall, stoutlooking student, as the Indian slid towards the
foot of the bed.

"Bleeding is manifestly and clearly indicated," retorted a bitter rival in love as well as medicine, "his
muscular action is too excessive," as Tubba made an in-
effectual effort to throw his body up to the top of the
mosquito bar.

"Bleeding would be as good as murder," said Number 1.

"Better cut his throat than stimulate him," said Number 2.

"Pshaw!"

"Fudge!"

"Sir!"

"Fellow!"

"Fool!"

"Liar!"

Vim! Vim! and stomach pump and brandy bottle flashed like meteors.

"Fight! fight! form a ring! fair play!"

"You're holding my friend."

"You lie! You rascal!"

Vim! Vim! from a new brace of combatants.

"He's gouging my brother! I must help! foul play!"

"Let go my hair!" Vim! Vim! and a triplet went at it.

I stopped rubbing and looked on with amazement. "Gentlemen, this is unprofessional! 'tis undignified! 'tis disgraceful! stop, I command you!" I yelled, but no one regarded me; some one struck me, and away I pitched into the whole lot promiscuously, having no partner, the patient dying on the bed whilst we were studying out his case.

"Fight! fight!" I heard yelled in the street, as I had finished giving a lick all round and could hardly keep from pitching into the mirror to whip up my reflection, I wanted a fight so badly.

"Fight! fight! in D[orsey]'s back office!" and here came the whole town to see the fun.

"I command the peace!" yelled Dick Locks; "I'm the mayor."

"And I'm the hoss for you!" screamed I, doubling him up with a lick in the stomach, which he replied to by laying me on my back, feeling very faint, in the opposite corner of the room.

"I command the peace!" continued Dick, flinging one of the combatants out of the window, another out of the door, and so on alternately until the peace was preserved by nearly breaking its infringers to pieces.

"What in the devil, Mr. Tensas, does this mean?" said my preceptor, who at that moment came in. "What does all this fighting and that drunken Indian lying in your bed mean? Have you all been drunk?"

"He has poisoned himself, sir, in my absence, with the Solution of Arsenic, which he took for whiskey; and as all the doctors were out of town, I called in the students, and they got to fighting over him whilst consulting," I replied, very indignantly, enraged at the insinuation that we had been drinking.

"Poisoned with Solution of Arsenic, ha! ha! oh! Lord! ha!" and my preceptor, throwing his burly form on the floor, rolled over and over, making the office ring with his laughter—"Poisoned, ha! ha!"

"Get out of this, you drunken rascal!" said he to the dying patient, applying his horsewhip to him vigorously. It acted like a charm: giving a loud yell of defiance, the old Choctaw sprang into the middle of the floor.

"Whoop! whiskey lour! Injun big man, drunk heap. Whoop! Tubba big Injun heap!" making tracks for the door and thence to the swamp.

The truth must out. The boys had got into the habit

of making too free with my preceptor's whiskey and
to keep off all but the knowing one he had labelled it
"Solution of Arsenic."

FROM *Louisiana Swamp Doctor: The Life and Writings*
of Henry Clay Lewis, edited by John Q. Anderson

Preface on Doctors
GEORGE BERNARD SHAW

It is not the fault of our doctors that the medical service of the community, as at present provided for, is a
murderous absurdity. That any sane nation, having observed that you could provide for the supply of bread
by giving bakers a pecuniary interest in baking for
you, should go on to give a surgeon a pecuniary interest
in cutting off your leg, is enough to make one despair
of political humanity. But that is precisely what we
have done. And the more appalling the mutilation, the
more the mutilator is paid. He who corrects the in-
growing toe-nail receives a few shillings: he who cuts
your inside out receives hundreds of guineas, except
when he does it to a poor person for practice.

Scandalized voices murmur that these operations are
necessary. They may be. It may also be necessary to
hang a man or pull down a house. But we take good
care not to make the hangman and the housebreaker
the judges of that. If we did, no man's neck would
be safe and no man's house stable. But we do make the
doctor the judge, and fine him anything from sixpence
to several hundred guineas if he decides in our favor.

I cannot knock my shins severely without forcing on some surgeon the difficult question, "Could I not make a better use of a pocketful of guineas than this man is making of his leg? Could he not write as well—or even better—on one leg than on two? And the guineas would make all the difference in the world to me just now. My wife—my pretty ones—the leg may mortify—it is always safer to operate—he will be well in a fortnight—artificial legs are now so well made that they are really better than natural ones—evolution is toward motors and leglessness, etc., etc., etc."

Now there is no calculation that an engineer can make as to the behavior of a girder under a strain, or an astronomer as to the recurrence of a comet, more certain than the calculation that under such circumstances we shall be dismembered unnecessarily in all directions by surgeons who believe the operations to be necessary solely because they want to perform them. The process metaphorically called bleeding the rich man is performed not only metaphorically but literally every day by surgeons who are quite as honest as most of us. After all, what harm is there in it? The surgeon need not take off the rich man's (or woman's) leg or arm: he can remove the appendix or the uvula, and leave the patient none the worse after a fortnight or so in bed, whilst the nurse, the general practitioner, the apothecary, and the surgeon will be the better.

Doubtful Character Borne by the Medical Profession

Again I hear the voices indignantly muttering old phrases about the high character of a noble profession and the honor and conscience of its members. I must

reply that the medical profession has not a high character; it has an infamous character. I do not know a single
thoughtful and well-informed person who does not
feel that the tragedy of illness at present is that it
delivers you helplessly into the hands of a profession
which you deeply mistrust, because it not only ad-
vocates and practises the most revolting cruelties in the
pursuit of knowledge, and justifies them on grounds
which would equally justify practising the same cruelties on yourself or your children, or burning down London to test a patent fire extinguisher, but, when it has
shocked the public, tries to reassure it with lies of
breath-bereaving brazenness. That is the character the
medical profession has got just now. It may be deserved
or it may not: there it is at all events, and the doctors
who have not realized this are living in a fool's paradise.
As to the honor and conscience of doctors, they have
as much as any other class of men, no more and no less.
And what other men dare pretend to be impartial
where they have a strong pecuniary interest on one
side? Nobody supposes that doctors are less virtuous
than judges; but a judge whose salary and reputation
depended on whether the verdict was for plaintiff or
defendant, prosecutor or prisoner, would be as little
trusted as a general in the pay of the enemy. To offer
me a doctor as my judge, and then weight his decision
with a bribe of a large sum of money and a virtual
guarantee that if he makes a mistake it can never be
proved against him, is to go wildly beyond the ascer-
tained strain which human nature will bear. It is simply
unscientific to allege or believe that doctors do not
under existing circumstances perform unnecessary op-

erations and manufacture and prolong lucrative illnesses. The only ones who can claim to be above suspicion are those who are so much sought after that their
cured patients are immediately replaced by fresh ones.
And there is this curious psychological fact to be remembered: a serious illness or a death advertizes the
doctor exactly as a hanging advertizes the barrister
who defended the person hanged. Suppose, for example, a royal personage gets something wrong with his
throat, or has a pain in his inside. If a doctor effects
some trumpery cure with a wet compress or a pepper-
mint lozenge nobody takes the least notice of him. But
if he operates on the throat and kills the patient, or extirpates an internal organ and keeps the whole nation
palpitating for days whilst the patient hovers in pain
and fever between life and death, his fortune is made:
every rich man who omits to call him in when the same
symptoms appear in his household is held not to have
done his utmost duty to the patient. The wonder is that
there is a king or queen left alive in Europe.

Doctors' Consciences

There is another difficulty in trusting to the honor
and conscience of a doctor. Doctors are just like other
Englishmen: most of them have no honor and no conscience: what they commonly mistake for these is sen-
timentality and an intense dread of doing anything that
everybody else does not do, or omitting to do anything
that everybody else does. This of course does amount to
a sort of working or rule-of-thumb conscience; but it
means that you will do anything, good or bad, provided you get enough people to keep you in coun-

tenance by doing it also. It is the sort of conscience that
makes it possible to keep order on a pirate ship, or in a
troop of brigands. It may be said that in the last analy-
sis there is no other sort of honor or conscience in
existence—that the assent of the majority is the only
sanction known to ethics. No doubt this holds good
in political practice. If mankind knew the facts, and
agreed with the doctors, then the doctors would be
in the right; and any person who thought otherwise
would be a lunatic. But mankind does not agree, and
does not know the facts. All that can be said for medical popularity is that until there is a practicable alternative to blind trust in the doctor, the truth about the
doctor is so terrible that we dare not face it. Molière
saw through the doctors; but he had to call them in just
the same. Napoleon had no illusions about them; but
he had to die under their treatment just as much as the
most credulous ignoramus that ever paid sixpence for
a bottle of strong medicine. In this predicament most
people, to save themselves from unbearable mistrust
and misery, or from being driven by their conscience
into actual conflict with the law, fall back on the old
rule that if you cannot have what you believe in you
must believe in what you have. When your child is ill
or your wife dying, and you happen to be very fond of
them, or even when, if you are not fond of them, you
are human enough to forget every personal grudge before the spectacle of a fellow creature in pain or peril,
what you want is comfort, reassurance, something to
clutch at, were it but a straw. This the doctor brings
you. You have a wildly urgent feeling that something
must be done; and the doctor does something. Some-

times what he does kills the patient; but you do not know that; and the doctor assures you that all that human skill could do has been done. And nobody has the brutality to say to the newly bereft father, mother, husband, wife, brother, or sister, "You have killed your lost darling by your credulity."

The Peculiar People

Besides, the calling in of the doctor is now compulsory except in cases where the patient is an adult and not too ill to decide the steps to be taken. We are subject to prosecution for manslaughter or for criminal neglect if the patient dies without the consolations of the medical profession. This menace is kept before the public by the Peculiar People. The Peculiars, as they are called, have gained their name by believing that the Bible is infallible, and taking their belief quite seriously. The Bible is very clear as to the treatment of illness. The Epistle of James, chapter v., contains the following explicit directions:—

> 14. Is any sick among you? let him call for the elders of the Church; and let them pray over him, anointing him with oil in the name of the Lord:
> 15. And the prayer of faith shall save the sick, and the Lord shall raise him up; and if he have committed sins, they shall be forgiven him.

The Peculiars obey these instructions and dispense with doctors. They are therefore prosecuted for manslaughter when their children die.

When I was a young man, the Peculiars were usually acquitted. The prosecution broke down when the doc-

tor in the witness box was asked whether, if the child
had had medical attendance, it would have lived. It
was, of course, impossible for any man of sense and
honor to assume divine omniscience by answering this
in the affirmative, or indeed pretending to be able to
answer it at all. And on this the judge had to instruct
the jury that they must acquit the prisoner. Thus a
judge with a keen sense of law (a very rare phenom-
enon on the Bench, by the way) was spared the possibility of having to sentence one prisoner (under the
Blasphemy Laws) for questioning the authority of
Scripture, and another for ignorantly and supersti-
tiously accepting it as a guide to conduct. Today all
this is changed. The doctor never hesitates to claim
divine omniscience, nor to clamor for laws to punish
any scepticism on the part of laymen. A modern doctor
thinks nothing of signing the death certificate of one of
his own diphtheria patients, and then going into the witness box and swearing a Peculiar into prison for six
months by assuring the jury, on oath, that if the prisoner's child, dead of diphtheria, had been placed under
his treatment instead of that of St. James, it would not
have died. And he does so not only with impunity, but
with public applause, though the logical course would
be to prosecute him either for the murder of his own
patient, or for perjury in the case of St. James. Yet no
barrister, apparently, dreams of asking for the statistics
of the relative case-mortality in diphtheria among the
Peculiars and among the believers in doctors, on which
alone any valid opinion could be founded. The barrister
is as superstitious as the doctor is infatuated; and the
Peculiar goes unpitied to his cell, though nothing what-

ever has been proved except that his child died without
the interference of a doctor as effectually as any of the
hundreds of children who die every day of the same
diseases in the doctor's care.

Recoil of the Dogma of Medical Infallibility on the Doctor

On the other hand, when the doctor is in the dock, or
is the defendant in an action for malpractice, he has to
struggle against the inevitable result of his former pre-
tences to infinite knowledge and unerring skill. He has
taught the jury and the judge, and even his own coun-
sel, to believe that every doctor can, with a glance at
the tongue, a touch on the pulse, and a reading of the
clinical thermometer, diagnose with absolute certainty
a patient's complaint, also that on dissecting a dead
body he can infallibly put his finger on the cause of
death, and, in cases where poisoning is suspected, the
nature of the poison used. Now all this supposed exact-
ness and infallibility is imaginary; and to treat a doctor
as if his mistakes were necessarily malicious or corrupt
malpractices (an inevitable deduction from the postu-
late that the doctor, being omniscient, cannot make
mistakes) is as unjust as to blame the nearest apothecary for not being prepared to supply you with six-
penny-worth of the elixir of life, or the nearest motor
garage for not having perpetual motion on sale in gal-
lon tins. But if apothecaries and motor car makers
habitually advertized elixir of life and perpetual motion, and succeeded in creating a strong general belief
that they could supply it, they would find themselves in
an awkward position if they were indicted for allowing

a customer to die, or for burning a chauffeur by putting
petrol into his car. That is the predicament the doctor
finds himself in when he has to defend himself against
a charge of malpractice by a plea of ignorance and fal-
libility. His plea is received with flat incredulity; and
he gets little sympathy, even from laymen who know,
because he has brought the incredulity on himself. If he
escapes, he can only do so by opening the eyes of the
jury to the facts that medical science is as yet very im-
perfectly differentiated from common curemongering
witchcraft; that diagnosis, though it means in many instances (including even the identification of patho-
genic bacilli under the microscope) only a choice
among terms so loose that they would not be accepted
as definitions in any really exact science, is, even at
that, an uncertain and difficult matter on which doctors
often differ; and that the very best medical opinion
and treatment varies widely from doctor to doctor, one
practitioner prescribing six or seven scheduled poi-
sons for so familiar a disease as enteric fever where another will not tolerate drugs at all; one starving a patient whom another would stuff; one urging an operation which another would regard as unnecessary and
dangerous; one giving alcohol and meat which another
would sternly forbid, etc., etc., etc.: all these discrepan-
cies arising not between the opinion of good doctors
and bad ones (the medical contention is, of course,
that a bad doctor is an impossibility), but between
practitioners of equal eminence and authority. Usually
it is impossible to persuade the jury that these facts are
facts. Juries seldom notice facts; and they have been
taught to regard any doubts of the omniscience and

omnipotence of doctors as blasphemy. Even the fact that doctors themselves die of the very diseases they profess to cure passes unnoticed. We do not shoot out our lips and shake our heads, saying, "They save others: themselves they cannot save": their reputation stands, like an African king's palace, on a foundation of dead bodies; and the result is that the verdict goes against the defendant when the defendant is a doctor accused of malpractice.

Fortunately for the doctors, they very seldom find themselves in this position, because it is so difficult to prove anything against them. The only evidence that can decide a case of malpractice is expert evidence: that is, the evidence of other doctors; and every doctor will allow a colleague to decimate a whole countryside sooner than violate the bond of professional etiquet by giving him away. It is the nurse who gives the doctor away in private, because every nurse has some particular doctor whom she likes; and she usually assures her patients that all the others are disastrous noodles, and soothes the tedium of the sick-bed by gossip about their blunders. She will even give a doctor away for the sake of making the patient believe that she knows more than the doctor. But she dare not, for her livelihood, give the doctor away in public. And the doctors stand by one another at all costs. Now and then some doctor in an unassailable position, like the late Sir William Gull, will go into the witness box and say what he really thinks about the way a patient has been treated; but such behavior is considered little short of infamous by his colleagues.

Why Doctors Do Not Differ

The truth is, there would never be any public agreement among doctors if they did not agree to agree on the main point of the doctor being always in the right. Yet the two guinea man never thinks that the five shilling man is right: if he did, he would be understood as confessing to an overcharge of £1:17s.; and on the same ground the five shilling man cannot encourage the notion that the owner of the sixpenny surgery round the corner is quite up to his mark. Thus even the layman has to be taught that infallibility is not quite infallible, because there are two qualities of it to be had at two prices.

But there is no agreement even in the same rank at the same price. During the first great epidemic of influenza towards the end of the nineteenth century a London evening paper sent round a journalist-patient to all the great consultants of that day, and published their advice and prescriptions: a proceeding passionately denounced by the medical papers as a breach of confidence of these eminent physicians. The case was the same; but the prescriptions were different, and so was the advice. Now a doctor cannot think his own treatment right and at the same time think his colleague right in prescribing a different treatment when the patient is the same. Anyone who has ever known doctors well enough to hear medical shop talked without reserve knows that they are full of stories about each other's blunders and errors, and that the theory of their omniscience and omnipotence no more holds good among themselves than it did with Molière and

Napoleon. But for this very reason no doctor dare accuse another of malpractice. He is not sure enough of his own opinion to ruin another man by it. He knows that if such conduct were tolerated in his profession no doctor's livelihood or reputation would be worth a year's purchase. I do not blame him: I should do the same myself. But the effect of this state of things is to make the medical profession a conspiracy to hide its own shortcomings. No doubt the same may be said of all professions. They are all conspiracies against the laity; and I do not suggest that the medical conspiracy is either better or worse than the military conspiracy, the legal conspiracy, the sacerdotal conspiracy, the pedagogic conspiracy, the royal and aristocratic conspiracy, the literary and artistic conspiracy, and the innumerable industrial, commercial, and financial conspiracies, from the trade unions to the great exchanges, which make up the huge conflict which we call society. But it is less suspected. The Radicals who used to advocate, as an indispensable preliminary to social reform, the strangling of the last king with the entrails of the last priest, substituted compulsory vaccination for compulsory baptism without a murmur.

The Craze for Operations

Thus everything is on the side of the doctor. When men die of disease they are said to die from natural causes. When they recover (and they mostly do) the doctor gets the credit of curing them. In surgery all operations are recorded as successful if the patient can be got out of the hospital or nursing home alive, though the subsequent history of the case may be such as would make an honest surgeon vow never to recommend or perform the operation again. The large range of operations which consist of amputating limbs and extirpating organs admits of no direct verification of their necessity. There is a fashion in operations as there is in sleeves and skirts: the triumph of some surgeon who has at last found out how to make a once desperate operation fairly safe is usually followed by a rage for that operation not only among the doctors, but actually among their patients. There are men and women whom the operating table seems to fascinate: half-alive people who through vanity, or hypochondria, or a craving to be the constant objects of anxious attention or what not, lose such feeble sense as they ever had of the value of their own organs and limbs. They seem to care as little for mutilation as lobsters or lizards, which at least have the excuse that they grow new claws and new tails if they lose the old ones. Whilst this book was being prepared for the press a case was tried in the Courts, of a man who sued a railway company for damages because a train had run over him and amputated both his legs. He lost his case because it was proved that he had deliberately contrived the occurrence himself for the sake of getting an idler's pension at the expense of the railway company, being too dull to realize how much more he had to lose than to gain by the bargain even if he had won his case and received damages above his utmost hopes.

This amazing case makes it possible to say, with some prospect of being believed, that there is in the classes who can afford to pay for fashionable operations a sprinkling of persons so incapable of appreciating the relative importance of preserving their bodily integrity (including the capacity for parentage) and the pleasure of talking about themselves and hearing themselves talked about as the heroes and heroines of sensational operations, that they tempt surgeons to operate on them not only with huge fees, but with personal solicitation. Now it cannot be too often repeated that when an operation is once performed, nobody can ever prove that it was unnecessary. If I refuse to allow my leg to be amputated, its mortification and my death may prove that I was wrong; but if I let the leg go, nobody can ever prove that it would not have mortified had I been obstinate. Operation is therefore the safe side for the surgeon as well as the lucrative side. The result is that we hear of "conservative surgeons" as a distinct class of practitioners who make it a rule not to operate if they can possibly help it, and who are sought after by the people who have vitality enough to regard an operation as a last resort. But no surgeon is bound to take the conservative view. If he believes that an organ is at best a useless survival, and that if he extirpates it the patient will be well and none the worse in a fortnight, whereas to await the natural cure would mean a month's illness, then he is clearly justified in recommending the operation even if the cure without operation is as certain as anything of the kind ever can be. Thus the conservative surgeon and the radical or extirpatory surgeon may both be right as far as the ultimate cure is concerned; so that their consciences do not help them out of their differences.

Credulity and Chloroform

There is no harder scientific fact in the world than the fact that belief can be produced in practically unlimited quantity and intensity, without observation or reasoning, and even in defiance of both, by the simple desire to believe founded on a strong interest in believing. Everybody recognizes this in the case of the amatory infatuations of the adolescents who see angels and heroes in obviously (to others) commonplace and even objectionable maidens and youths. But it holds good over the entire field of human activity. The hardest-headed materialist will become a consulter of table-rappers and slate-writers if he loses a child or a wife so beloved that the desire to revive and communicate with them becomes irresistible. The cobbler believes that there is nothing like leather. The Imperialist who regards the conquest of England by a foreign power as the worst of political misfortunes believes that the conquest of a foreign power by England would be a boon to the conquered. Doctors are no more proof against such illusions than other men. Can anyone then doubt that under existing conditions a great deal of unnecessary and mischievous operating is bound to go on, and that patients are encouraged to imagine that modern surgery and anesthesia have made operations much less serious matters than they really are? When doctors write or speak to the public about operations, they imply, and often say in so many words, that chloroform has made surgery painless. People who have been operated on know better. The patient does not feel the knife, and the operation is therefore enormously facilitated for the surgeon; but the patient pays for the anesthesia with hours of wretched sickness; and when that is over there is the pain of the wound made by the surgeon, which has to heal like any other wound. This is why operating surgeons, who are usually out of the house with their fee in their pockets before the patient has recovered consciousness, and who therefore see nothing of the suffering witnessed by the general practitioner and the nurse, occasionally talk of operations very much as the hangman in Barnaby Rudge talked of executions, as if being operated on were a luxury in sensation as well as in price.

Medical Poverty

To make matters worse, doctors are hideously poor. The Irish gentleman doctor of my boyhood, who took nothing less than a guinea, though he might pay you four visits for it, seems to have no equivalent nowadays in English society. Better be a railway porter than an ordinary English general practitioner. A railway porter has from eighteen to twenty-three shillings a week from the Company merely as a retainer; and his additional fees from the public, if we leave the third-class two-penny tip out of account (and I am by no means sure that even this reservation need be made), are equivalent to doctor's fees in the case of second-class passengers, and double doctor's fees in the case of first. Any class of educated men thus treated tends to become a brigand class, and doctors are no exception to the rule. They are offered disgraceful prices for advice and medicine. Their patients are for the most part so poor and so ignorant that good advice would be re-

sented as impracticable and wounding. When you are
so poor that you cannot afford to refuse eighteenpence
from a man who is too poor to pay you any more, it is
useless to tell him that what he or his sick child needs is
not medicine, but more leisure, better clothes, better
food, and a better drained and ventilated house. It is
kinder to give him a bottle of something almost as
cheap as water, and tell him to come again with another eighteenpence if it does not cure him. When you
have done that over and over again every day for a
week, how much scientific conscience have you left? If
you are weak-minded enough to cling desperately to
your eighteenpence as denoting a certain social supe-
riority to the sixpenny doctor, you will be miserably
poor all your life; whilst the sixpenny doctor, with his
low prices and quick turnover of patients, visibly makes
much more than you do and kills no more people.

A doctor's character can no more stand out against
such conditions than the lungs of his patients can stand
out against bad ventilation. The only way in which he
can preserve his self-respect is by forgetting all he ever
learnt of science, and clinging to such help as he can
give without cost merely by being less ignorant and
more accustomed to sick-beds than his patients. Finally,
he acquires a certain skill at nursing cases under poverty-
stricken domestic conditions, just as women who have
been trained as domestic servants in some huge institution with lifts, vacuum cleaners, electric lighting,
steam heating, and machinery that turns the kitchen into
a laboratory and engine house combined, manage, when
they are sent out into the world to drudge as general
servants, to pick up their business in a new way, learn-

ing the slatternly habits and wretched makeshifts of homes where even bundles of kindling wood are luxuries to be anxiously economized.

The Successful Doctor

The doctor whose success blinds public opinion to medical poverty is almost as completely demoralized. His promotion means that his practice becomes more and more confined to the idle rich. The proper advice for most of their ailments is typified in Abernethy's "Live on sixpence a day and earn it." But here, as at the other end of the scale, the right advice is neither agreeable nor practicable. And every hypochondriacal rich lady or gentleman who can be persuaded that he or she is a lifelong invalid means anything from fifty to five hundred pounds a year for the doctor. Operations enable a surgeon to earn similar sums in a couple of hours; and if the surgeon also keeps a nursing home, he may make considerable profits at the same time by running what is the most expensive kind of hotel. These gains are so great that they undo much of the moral advantage which the absence of grinding pecuniary anxiety gives the rich doctor over the poor one. It is true that the temptation to prescribe a sham treatment because the real treatment is too dear for either patient or doctor does not exist for the rich doctor. He always has plenty of genuine cases which can afford genuine treatment; and these provide him with enough sincere scientific professional work to save him from the ignorance, obsolescence, and atrophy of scientific conscience into which his poorer colleagues sink. But on the other hand his expenses are enormous. Even as a

bachelor, he must, at London west end rates, make over
a thousand a year before he can afford even to insure
his life. His house, his servants, and his equipage (or
autopage) must be on the scale to which his patients
are accustomed, though a couple of rooms with a camp
bed in one of them might satisfy his own requirements.
Above all, the income which provides for these out-
goings stops the moment he himself stops working.
Unlike the man of business, whose managers, clerks,
warehousemen and laborers keep his business going
whilst he is in bed or in his club, the doctor cannot earn
a farthing by deputy. Though he is exceptionally exposed to infection, and has to face all weathers at all
hours of the night and day, often not enjoying a complete night's rest for a week, the money stops coming
in the moment he stops going out; and therefore illness
has special terrors for him, and success no certain
permanence. He dare not stop making hay while the
sun shines; for it may set at any time. Men do not resist
pressure of this intensity. When they come under it as
doctors they pay unnecessary visits; they write prescriptions that are as absurd as the rub of chalk with which
an Irish tailor once charmed away a wart from my
father's finger; they conspire with surgeons to promote
operations; they nurse the delusions of the *malade
imaginaire* (who is always really ill because, as there
is no such thing as perfect health, nobody is ever
really well); they exploit human folly, vanity, and fear
of death as ruthlessly as their own health, strength, and
patience are exploited by selfish hypochondriacs. They
must do all these things or else run pecuniary risks that
no man can fairly be asked to run. And the healthier

the world becomes, the more they are compelled to live by imposture and the less by that really helpful activity of which all doctors get enough to preserve them from utter corruption. For even the most hardened humbug who ever prescribed ether tonics to ladies whose need for tonics is of precisely the same character as the need of poorer women for a glass of gin, has to help a mother through child-bearing often enough to feel that he is not living wholly in vain.

FROM *The Doctor's Dilemma*

The Soldier Who Saw Everything Twice
JOSEPH HELLER

Yossarian owed his good health to exercise, fresh air, teamwork and good sportsmanship; it was to get away from them all that he had first discovered the hospital. When the physical-education officer at Lowery Field ordered everyone to fall out for calisthenics one afternoon, Yossarian, the private, reported instead at the dispensary with what he said was a pain in his right side.

"Beat it," said the doctor on duty there, who was doing a crossword puzzle.

"We can't tell him to beat it," said a corporal. "There's a new directive about abdominal complaints. We have to keep them under observation five days because so many of them have been dying after we make them beat it."

"All right," grumbled the doctor. "Keep him under observation five days and *then* make him beat it."

They took Yossarian's clothes away and put him in a ward, where he was very happy when no one was snoring nearby. In the morning a helpful young English intern popped in to ask him about his liver.

"I think it's my appendix that's bothering me," Yossarian told him.

"Your appendix is no good," the Englishman declared with jaunty authority. "If your appendix goes wrong, we can take it out and have you back on active duty in almost no time at all. But come to us with a liver complaint and you can fool us for weeks. The liver, you see, is a large, ugly mystery to us. If you've ever eaten liver you know what I mean. We're pretty sure today that the liver exists, and we have a fairly good idea of what it does whenever it's doing what it's supposed to be doing. Beyond that, we're really in the dark. After all, what is a liver? My father, for example, died of cancer of the liver and was never sick a day of his life right up till the moment it killed him. Never felt a twinge of pain. In a way, that was too bad, since I hated my father. Lust for my mother, you know."

"What's an English medical officer doing on duty here?" Yossarian wanted to know.

The officer laughed. "I'll tell you all about that when I see you tomorrow morning. And now throw that silly ice bag away before you die of pneumonia."

Yossarian never saw him again. That was one of the nice things about all the doctors at the hospital; he never saw any of them a second time. They came and went and simply disappeared. In place of the English intern the next day, there arrived a group of doctors he had never seen before to ask him about his appendix.

"There's nothing wrong with my appendix," Yossarian informed them. "The doctor yesterday said it was my liver."

"Maybe it is his liver," replied the white-haired officer in charge. "What does his blood count show?"

"He hasn't had a blood count."

"Have one taken right away. We can't afford to take chances with a patient in his condition. We've got to keep ourselves covered in case he dies." He made a notation on his clipboard and spoke to Yossarian. "In the meantime, keep that ice bag on. It's very important."

"I don't have an ice bag on."

"Well, get one. There must be an ice bag around here somewhere. And let someone know if the pain becomes unendurable."

At the end of ten days, a new group of doctors came to Yossarian with bad news: he was in perfect health and had to get out. He was rescued in the nick of time by a patient across the aisle who began to see everything twice. Without warning, the patient sat up in bed and shouted,

"I see everything twice!"

A nurse screamed and an orderly fainted. Doctors came running up from every direction with needles, lights, tubes, rubber mallets and oscillating metal tines. They rolled up complicated instruments on wheels. There was not enough of the patient to go around, and specialists pushed forward in line with raw tempers and snapped at their colleagues in front to hurry up and give somebody else a chance. A colonel with a large forehead and horn-rimmed glasses soon arrived at a diagnosis.

"It's meningitis," he called out emphatically, waving the others back. "Although Lord knows there's not the slightest reason for thinking so."

"Then why pick meningitis?" inquired a major with a suave chuckle. "Why not, let's say, acute nephritis?"

"Because I'm a meningitis man, that's why, and not an acute-nephritis man," retorted the colonel. "And I'm not going to give him up to any of you kidney birds without a struggle. I was here first."

In the end, the doctors were all in accord. They agreed they had no idea what was wrong with the soldier who saw everything twice, and they rolled him away into a room in the corridor and quarantined everyone else in the ward for fourteen days.

Thanksgiving Day came and went without any fuss while Yossarian was still in the hospital. The only bad thing about it was the turkey for dinner, and even that was pretty good. It was the most rational Thanksgiving he had ever spent, and he took a sacred oath to spend every future Thanksgiving Day in the cloistered shelter of a hospital. He broke his sacred oath the very next year, when he spent the holiday in a hotel room instead in intellectual conversation with Lieutenant Scheisskopf's wife. . . .

That was the most illogical Thanksgiving he could ever remember spending, and his thoughts returned wishfully to his halcyon fourteen-day quarantine in the hospital the year before; but even that idyll had ended on a tragic note: he was still in good health when the quarantine period was over, and they told him again that he had to get out and go to war. Yossarian sat up in bed when he heard the bad news and shouted,

"I see everything twice!"

Pandemonium broke loose in the ward again. The specialists came running up from all directions and ringed him in a circle of scrutiny so confining that he could feel the humid breath from their various noses blowing uncomfortably upon the different sectors of his body. They went snooping into his eyes and ears with tiny beams of light, assaulted his legs and feet with rubber hammers and vibrating forks, drew blood from his veins, held anything handy up for him to see on the periphery of his vision.

The leader of this team of doctors was a dignified, solicitous gentleman who held one finger up directly in front of Yossarian and demanded, "How many fingers do you see?"

"Two," said Yossarian.

"How many fingers do you see now?" asked the doctor, holding up two.

"Two," said Yossarian.

"And how many now?" asked the doctor, holding up none.

"Two," said Yossarian.

The doctor's face wreathed with a smile. "By Jove, he's right," he declared jubilantly. "He *does* see everything twice."

They rolled Yossarian away on a stretcher into the room with the other soldier who saw everything twice and quarantined everyone else in the ward for another fourteen days.

"I see everything twice!" the soldier who saw everything twice shouted when they rolled Yossarian in.

"I see everything twice!" Yossarian shouted back at him just as loudly, with a secret wink.

"The walls! The walls!" the other soldier cried. "Move back the walls!"

"The walls! The walls!" Yossarian cried. "Move back the walls!"

One of the doctors pretended to shove the wall back. "Is that far enough?"

The soldier who saw everything twice nodded weakly and sank back on his bed. Yossarian nodded weakly too, eying his talented roommate with great humility and admiration. He knew he was in the presence of a master. His talented roommate was obviously a person to be studied and emulated. During the night, his talented roommate died, and Yossarian decided that he had followed him far enough.

"I see everything once!" he cried quickly.

A new group of specialists came pounding up to his bedside with their instruments to find out if it was true.

"How many fingers do you see?" asked the leader, holding up one.

"One."

The doctor held up two fingers. "How many fingers do you see now?"

"One."

The doctor held up ten fingers. "And how many now?"

"One."

The doctor turned to the other doctors with amazement. "He *does* see everything once!" he exclaimed. "We made him all better."

FROM *Catch-22*

CHAPTER II

What Blue Cross Doesn't Tell You

Now that you have glimpsed some of medicine's hilarious history, you will find it easier to understand how it got the way it is today. With modern medical science's dazzling array of technology and technique, new cures are being discovered almost as rapidly as new diseases. New and better antibiotics are being invented to help cope with the sometimes awful effects of the old antibiotics. New television series have refurbished the traditional doctor-image, and the AMA is waging a large-scale public relations war to maintain that image while simultaneously quashing socialized medicine. The next four selections offer spot-checks on these and other areas of modern medicine.

An Ordeal to Choke a Sword-Swallower

SHANA ALEXANDER

Although I am otherwise reasonably healthy, there is something about Christmas that always makes me get sick. Last year it was a backache, the year before an earache—my annual Wassail collapse is becoming a family tradition. This past Christmas I overreached myself and wound up not only sick in bed but upside down and miserable as well. My own description of my symptoms sounded to me like the label off a patent-medicine bottle. The main complaint was an off-and-on unexplained cough I've had for seven years, and the upshot of my talks with several doctors was to go to the hospital so that definitive tests could be made.

In case you missed the bronchoscopy and the bronchogram on *Dr. Kildare*, what it means is that first they slide a metal tube with a light on the end of it down into your windpipe in order to examine your lungs in living color. Later they get you to inhale a couple of lungfuls of thick, white, luminous goo that shows up in incredibly detailed X rays which make your chest look like something that should be on display at Marineland.

The procedure is a hospital commonplace, but it can require a lot of fuss, and—should the patient turn out to have both a very powerful gag reflex and large front

teeth (I could have told them if someone had bothered
to ask)—it may also involve quite a crescendo of drugs.
My own recollection, as clearly as I can remember it,
is of an oratorio for massed barbiturates, and my brains
felt scrambled for weeks afterward. It was an ordeal
to befuddle a hophead and choke a sword-swallower,
and, though I now do know what was causing my cough
(nothing too serious), I wasn't sure until this morning
that I would ever fully get over the tests.

The patient is of course warned that the tests are
going to make him feel bad. Part of the recommended
post-hospital therapy is to spend as much time as possible lying on a slant board, feet 15 inches higher than
head. Although medicine calls this "postural drainage,"
Elizabeth Arden calls the same thing "the beauty angle," so I figured it couldn't be too unpleasant. I bor-
rowed a board from a ladies' gym, set it in front of the
TV set, clambered on, wrapped myself tightly in a
blanket to ward off chilly floor-level drafts, hooked my
wrapped feet under the ankle strap and slowly let myself lie back. This posture is ideal for being fired into
orbit or buried at sea, but it turns out to be useless for
anything else, including reading, TV or even light conversation. When lying at floor level and upside down
on the dining room floor, the first thing that drains
away is social aplomb. One becomes a sort of elongated
hassock for children and dogs to trip over and, since
one has, after all, "passed" the dreaded tests, there is
not even much sympathy to be garnered from clucking
friends. All in all, there has been plenty of time to think
in the past few weeks, and my thoughts were surely

stimulated by the rush of blood to the head. What I thought about of course was me and doctors.

It was a 24-hour theme and I couldn't turn it off. At night I had grotesque dreams straight out of oldtime vaudeville: terrified patient strapped onto operating table: "Doctor, I'm dubious." Doctor (leering): "Glad to meet you, Mr. Dubious." (Followed by loud clanking of tire irons, hacksaws and other surgical gear.)

By day, when vertical, I hunted out medical stories in the newspapers. One I remember vividly was a front-page announcement of some research by a couple of distinguished social scientists who warned that TV shows like *Ben Casey* and *Dr. Kildare* were doing serious damage to the American doctor image. By portraying the physician not as kindly, wise, white-haired old Dr. Christian but as a human being who gets hungry and sleepy and even sometimes makes mistakes, TV was accused of helping to destroy the awe, the charisma, the "social distance" which is vital to the doctor-patient relationship. Though upside down, I was still dubious. Certainly faith is important and itself therapeutic, but my faith is always stronger in the mortal man than in the high priest, however glittery his charisma or white his hair. Or at least that is the case when I am vertical. The difficulty with becoming a patient is that as soon as you get horizontal, part of you begins yearning not for a mortal doctor but for a medicine man.

The real trouble with the doctor image in America is that it has been grayed by the image of the doctor-as-businessman, the doctor-as-bureaucrat, the doctor-as-medical-robot, and the doctor-as-terrified-victim-of-malpractice-suits. I have no suggestions as to what the medical profession as a whole can do about this; it may be a matter for each doctor to grapple with individually. The one doctor I know of to have materially improved his or her image is a lady pediatrician who got so mad at her office medical linen service (she had just been accused of the theft of 700 towels) that in a fury she canceled the service and bought a black uniform. She decorated this with bright felt cutouts of hearts and flowers, and sewed a big red lollipop up the back. She says her patients love her new image, and so do I.

I would not think of having a doctor I didn't like. The reason has nothing to do with his professional competence, which I cannot judge anyhow. My liking him won't make him a better doctor, but I think it will make me a better patient.

I don't require him to have a lollipop up his back, but I do want my doctor to listen very carefully to what I have to say: to tell me every bit he can about what he is looking for and what he finds: and when he doesn't know, say so.

One day last week I got up off the board and found to my horror that I could hardly move my neck. I seemed to be wearing a high, choked collar of painful swollen glands. My first thought was that all the poison had drained out of my lungs and back into my neck. This odd new symptom, coming after all my other complaints, made me fear that the real trouble must be flaming hypochondria. But, I reminded myself, I *like* my doctor and, after all, I couldn't move my neck. It was last Friday by the time he had checked out this new complaint and called back to say he thought it probably was some sort of virus. The board had nothing to do with it. "Let me know Monday how you are," he said—"as for treatment, I have absolutely nothing to suggest."

My neck and I did spend a rather uncomfortable weekend together, but I did nothing about it. When I called my doctor today, his office was humming with a new crop of Monday morning patients, so I just left a message with the nurse: Mrs. Alexander feels fine.

FROM *Life*, January 21, 1966

Silver Lining

R. G. G. PRICE

It is easy for newspaper readers to feel selfish delight when they read cheerful pieces about the progress of curative medicine and forget that it is only the tireless ingenuity in the invention of new diseases that keeps the medical and pharmaceutical boys ahead of the game. They have taken some nasty knocks since Jenner slashed their income from smallpox-treatment fees. This century it is only the brilliance of such happy strokes of popularization as cardiac infarction, protruded disk, anxiety state, and night starvation that has kept doctors and drug makers up the greasy pole of the income table.

At one time, pessimists thought sulfonamides and

antibiotics would reduce doctors to the status of village blacksmiths. Not a bit of it! Antibiotic-resistant viruses were discovered right on time, and before long even less domesticated micro-organisms may be brought back from space, particularly when some of the less enthusiastically hygienic nations get into the act. And there is another direction in which advance has been dramatic. The more weapons against infective disease that the spoilsports discover, the more psychosomatic conditions are brought in to fill the financial gap— more than fill it, in fact. The good old family physician might cure a pneumonia in less than a dozen visits. The specialist in health-through-conversation can take as long as the traffic will bear and make patients come to him instead of having to turn out into the snowy night.

One of the brightest strokes of imagination of recent years was drug allergy. You cured the complaint but still had the patient to treat for the effects of the cure. Probably some forward-looking lab is busy working on skin conditions produced by fear of being allergic to antibiotics.

As any issue of the *Reader's Digest* will show, the doctors and the drug houses suffer a pretty steady stream of defeats. They have to keep on their toes if cures aren't to outnumber diseases, with appalling economic consequences. It is easy enough for patients to take the troubles of their advisers and suppliers with unsympathetic grins. But medicine and surgery and miscellaneous therapeutics and putting minute quantities of powerful compounds in capsules and thinking of fresh claims to make for them and building new wings onto hospitals play a major part in a national economy. Any serious danger to disease is more than just a headache for a handful of corporations and occupational groups; it is a blow at a country's financial solar plexus.

I have mentioned viruses of stellar or planetary origin: but there is, of course, a danger that astronauts might find an elixir of life, or a universal nostrum just growing wild, or even some kind of plankton that cured the common cold. If this seems unlikely, remember that the medieval barber-surgeon pottered around with his lancet, his bowl, and perhaps a pouch of leeches, never realizing, happy man, that not far ahead in terms of historical time Pasteur lay in wait. I don't know enough about insurance to say whether future-minded men and institutions are already taking out policies against the discovery of a simple and cheap cure for schizophrenia or arthritis or mother fixation or influenza.

What lines are the creative people going to be working on in the next few years? One is certainly going to be linking vague but credible symptoms to inescapable environmental conditions. We have already seen some ingenious use of motoring and television. However much driving and viewing may constrict stomach muscles, strain eyes, distort digestive processes, and allow fat to silt up arteries for lack of exercise, there is little fear that people are going to give them up. But modern life consists of more than cars and TV sets. Tower blocks can be accused of leading to eardrum degeneration, owing to constant use of high-speed elevators, without any risk of a return to lots of little low-built homes in gardens. Air travel may produce spinal tensions due to boredom, but flying is here to stay. Children need not be left out: obsession with space exploration could lead to a pediatric gold mine—reverse numeracy, where the sufferer counts backward. Man is going to go on taking pharmaceutical products, so there is a profitable future in the side effects arising from consumption of whatever it is capsules are made of.

The old family doctor who would tackle anything is being superseded by narrow specialists. This has a profitable result: each consultant can blame the previous consultant's cures—for example, a malfunctioning digestive system can be attributed to defects in an ophthalmologist's prescription. Psychiatrists, whose prosperity is built on persuading patients that they are not guilty and transferring the guilt to non-patients, often now in the family vault, can make good use of disease phobias caused by excessively elaborate check-ups —caused by almost anything medical, in fact, except, of course, heavy bills. On this point doctors stand shoulder to shoulder, and the highest standard of medical ethics is maintained.

Looking into the future, what does the prophetic pathologist see? Not, surely, a race of happy gods, unanxious and committed to a healthful diet. The prophet is, after all, human himself, and it is man's innate, and often apparently unfounded, optimism that has kept his head above water. Nature, he must feel, generally has something profitable up its sleeve. There is, for example, a rumor of a new ice age, and cold weather means chilblains.

FROM *Atlantic*, October 1966

Is It Fatal, Doc?

ARTHUR HOPPE

I've been having this pain. Right here. So naturally I
called up my lovable old family physician, Doc Christian, whose dedication and selflessness, night and day,
year in and year out . . . Only I had to wait a week
for an appointment because Doc was down at the AMA
Convention, passing resolutions.

But when I did get in, I felt a sense of security.
There was the same old black couch, the same old
hooked rug, the same old tatted mottoes hanging from
the wall. Like: STAMP OUT SOCIALIZED MEDICINE.

On the battered old end table by the battered old
straight-backed chair lay the same battered old magazines with the same battered old articles I had read so
many times before: "Government Health Insurance
and Other Cancers" and "Can Socialized Medicine
Cure Gallstones?"

I found old Doc back in his office, seated at his lovable old roll-top desk. He was just the same: bushy
white hair, rimless glasses perched on the end of his
nose, graying mustache drooping over the corners of
his kindly mouth. Doc's more than a doctor to us folks
around here. He's a homey philosopher, a wise coun-
selor, a true friend in our hour of trouble.

"Doc," I said, "I've got this pain . . ."

He looked up at me over his glasses, shook his shaggy
head sadly and said: "Creeping paralysis."

I blanched. "Doc," I asked nervously, "are you sure?"

"No question about it," he said. I could tell he hated the thought as much as I. "The symptoms are unmistakable."

I sought desperately in my mind for some ray of hope. But I couldn't remember old Doc ever being wrong. Except for that hysterectomy on George, the mailman. "How long?" I asked, striving to keep my voice even.

"It could happen tomorrow," he said. "But if you help me fight it, maybe we can lick this thing together."

That's good old Doc, great on psychology. "What can I do?" I asked eagerly.

With the solemnity that instills confidence, Doc reached for his battered old black bag. Just the sight of it reassured me. Ah, the wondrous cures he has pulled from its depths over the years. It had become the symbol of old Doc and the selfless interest he takes in each of us folks who depend so on his advice and guidance.

"First," he said, all businesslike as always, "take these." And he drew forth from the old black bag a petition to the President, four mimeographed press releases, and the full text of an address entitled: "Socialized Medicine Means the Creeping Paralysis for Our Socio-Economic Order."

"Write your congressman daily and see your senator twice a year," said Doc. "Ten dollars, please."

So I'm awfully busy these days organizing Mothers' Marches to Fight Creeping Paralysis and what not. But it's worth it. As Doc says: "You let the government stick its nose into private medicine and the old family physician is going to get all messed up in politics."

And I don't know what us folks around here would do if old Doc got all messed up in politics. Who'd take care of us?

I just wish this pain would go away. It's right here. No, a little higher.

I mention the pain occasionally to old Doc. I tell him I've digested all the brochures he prescribed. The last time I saw him—it was just before he went on strike—he smiled his kindly old smile and gave me, free of charge, a new miracle pamphlet in capsule form. Called: *It's a Dirty Lie.*

This is about the dedicated doctors who are now signing pledges not to treat elderly patients under the benefits of the King-Anderson Bill. Should the bill ever get through Congress. And it points out righteously that these dedicated doctors will instead treat these elderly patients absolutely free as charity cases. In order to preserve the sacred right of every indigent American to be cared for in the charity ward of his own choice.

Well, I know all us folks around here agree that good old Doc knows what's best for us, politically speaking. But I'm a mite anxious to see how the AMA's big battle will affect our television programs. Like:

(Scene: The operating room of Big City General. The gleaming corropulator scintillates monotonously. In-out; in-out. The sederath pulsator pulsates with reas-

suring regularity. Up-down; up-down. The dedicated
young interne, Dr. Ben Caseless, bends intently over
the swathed form of the patient as his mentor, wise old
Dr. A. M. A. Gilseppi, his wise old smile hidden behind
his wise old mask, watches closely.)

DR. CASELESS (*tensely*): Sponge . . . form letter to
my congressman . . . hemostat . . . press release . . .
tire spanner . . .

DR. GILSEPPI (*smiling wisely*): So far, so good, Doctor.
But now the ticklish part. You must ever so carefully
incise the obsidized lobe of the anterior ventricle with
your left hand while signing postcards to your precinct
with the other.

DR. CASELESS (*sweating*): It's not easy, Doctor, to be a
good doctor. But I think . . . Yes, I've got it.

DR. GILSEPPI (*examining the postcards*): A few minor
mistakes, Doctor. But you may make a doctor yet, Doctor. The rest is, of course, routine. You enter the duo-
denum, turn left at the pancreas, underpass the kidney, and remove the patient's wallet.

DR. CASELESS (*laughing*): Gosh, Doctor, we learned
that in first-year med.

(*Humming happily, he follows the proper route and
finally extracts the wallet. As he holds it up, the corropulator scintillates wildly and the sederath pulsifies
like a thing gone mad. Up-out-in-down-up!*)

DR. CASELESS (*horrified*): Doctor! A crisis! I can't go on.
There's been a terrible mistake in Admissions. This
isn't a Blue Cross patient. His wallet is not only in-
fected with a Social Security card, but—ugh!—he's

got a certificate for benefits under the King-Anderson Bill! It's a terminal case.

DR. GILSEPPI (*gripping the younger man's shoulder*): Doctor! Pull yourself together. We men of medicine must never give up hope in our fight to preserve the sacred right of the physician to choose his own patient. After all, son, it takes more than a knowledge of pills to make a good doctor. You need a heap of understanding too, son, of politics.

DR. CASELESS: But, Doctor, the ravages of socialism in this patient have gone too far to . . .

(*Wise old Dr. Gilseppi merely smiles wisely, picks up a scalpel and performs a neat prefrontal lobotomy with his right hand while dashing off a telegram to his senator with his left. Dr. Caseless shakes his head in smiling awe at the wisdom of his old mentor as the corropulator and sederath resume their reassuring beat and the curtain falls.*)

FROM *The Love Everybody Crusade*

The Miracle Drugs Abroad
ART BUCHWALD

Some time ago the American boss of a friend of mine told the friend, "I admire you people who live abroad. You don't take pills. In America we're always taking a pill for something or other. We're becoming a nation of hypochondriacs. But you people here don't depend on pills."

My friend agreed. "We can't get any."

Well, it was a good story, but not necessarily true. The majority of Americans coming to Europe are weighted down with every imaginable medication prescribed by family doctors. Each one is a miracle drug in its own right, and I haven't met an American tourist yet who isn't willing to share his medicines with the less fortunate people who live abroad.

Just recently I had the occasion to see how many Americans will come to the aid of their fellow men. It all started off when I complained at a dinner party of having a sore throat.

"I have just the thing for you," the hostess said. "It's Slipawhizdrene. You take one every two hours."

One of the guests said, "Slipawhizdrene is outdated. My doctor gave me Heventizeall. It doesn't make you as sleepy, and you only have to take two every four hours."

"I left the United States two weeks after you did," another woman said, "and Heventizeall has been superseded by Deviltizeall. I have a bottle at the hotel, and if you stop by I'll give you some."

The only Frenchman at the table said, "Why don't you gargle with aspirin?"

The people at the dinner couldn't have been more shocked if he had said a four-letter word. The Frenchman's American wife was so embarrassed she almost broke into tears.

He looked around helplessly. "But what did I say wrong?"

The husband of the hostess tried to smooth things over. "You see, René, in America we have gone beyond aspirin. You French believe in food; we believe in miracle drugs."

"They're all barbarians," muttered one of the Americans.

After dinner I stopped by the hotel and picked up an envelope of Deviltizeall. I took two before I went to bed. At four in the morning I no longer had my sore throat, but I was violently sick to my stomach. I had a luncheon date with a Hollywood producer, but I couldn't eat anything.

"I've got just the thing for an upset stomach. It's called Egazzakine. Here, take one now, and one at four o'clock."

I took the proffered pill, and in a half-hour my stomach settled. Only now, my eyes started to run, and I began sneezing.

Making my way blindly to the office, I ran into another American friend in front of the Lancaster Hotel. He recognized the symptoms immediately. "You've probably got an allergy. Come upstairs and I'll give you something for it."

We went up to his room, and he took out a leather case filled with various bottles.

"Let's see," he said, reading from a slip of paper. "The yellow-and-black ones are for jaundice, the green-and-blue ones are for pneumonia, the white-and-red ones are for rheumatism, the pink-and-beige ones are for heart trouble—oh, yes, the brown-and-purple are for allergies. Here, take two now, and two at four o'clock."

"But," I protested, "I've got to take the Egazzakine at four o'clock."

"Don't do it," he warned. "That's what you're probably allergic to."

I took the brown-and-purple capsules and went to the office. In about an hour, my tear ducts had dried up and I had stopped sneezing.

I felt perfectly well, except I couldn't move my left arm.

I reported this to my friend at the Lancaster, who said, "The doctor warned me it happens sometimes. He gave me something else in case it did. I'll send it over with the bellboy."

The bellboy brought over some orange-and-cerise tablets.

I took two, and it wasn't long before I could lift my arm again.

That evening during dinner I discovered I had my sore throat back. But I didn't mention it to a soul.

FROM *Don't Forget to Write*

CHAPTER III

Post-Operative Hysteria

Given the nature and purpose of hospitals, it is somewhat strange that stories of operations and recuperations should so frequently abound in mirth. As anyone who has ever tried to tell about an impressive operation at a cocktail party can testify, everybody who is anybody has had absolutely the most fascinating operation on record, and one which was very likely followed by a recuperation of unremitting hilarity. Perhaps the intensely serious and soberly clinical attitude of hospital staffs is conducive to humor. Or perhaps we are simply more conscious of the comic in our nearer brushes with the tragic. Whatever the cause, however, we can be thankful for the effects, as represented here by the following three samples of hospital humor.

Operation Frame-up

CLAUDE BENJAMIN

"Bravo! Bravo!"

I modestly stepped away from the operating table and bowed.

"Encore! Encore!" pleaded the visiting dignitaries in the surgical amphitheatre.

I shrugged my shoulders. There was nothing left to remove because the body was empty. I took off my mask.

To a man they rose to their feet. "It's Claude Benjamin!" they buzzed.

The buzzing grew louder and louder until it was unbearable. I awakened from my dream with a start. It was the telephone. "Doctor Benjamin speaking," I said.

"Claude, this is Betty. I didn't wake you up, did I?"

"I've been up for hours," I yawned. "Looks like it's going to be a great day at the beach. What time do you want me to pick you up?"

"That's why I'm calling, Claude. Would you mind very much if I don't go with you this afternoon? I've been invited to the Navy Ball this evening and I don't want to be all sunburned."

I sat upright in bed. "But, Betty, I thought you had a date with me for the afternoon and evening."

"I'm sorry, but I promised Doctor Watson over two weeks ago."

"This is the third time this month you've stood me up for that stuffed shirt. Take away his Harvard accent, his elevator shoes and what have you got?"

"A lot of money," she whispered wickedly. "And he's very sexy."

"That heavy breathing isn't passion. It's adenoids!"

"I knew you'd understand. We'll have other days at the beach, but there's only one Navy Ball. 'Bye." She hung up.

So, Henry Watson thinks he can waltz off with my girl, does he. Well we'd see about that.

The phone rang again.

I laughed. I should have known she was just teasing me. She'd never break a date with me to go out with that drip. I picked up the receiver. "Thought you had me fooled, didn't you? Hello . . . What? Yes, this is Doctor Benjamin. The violent ward at the County Hospital? Now, why would anyone want me in the violent ward? Very funny, operator." She hung up cackling in my ear.

Ollie Anderson, male nurse in charge of the violent ward, peeped at me through the reinforced glass window, then unlocked the steel door. "Your old drinking partner's been asking for you, Doctor Benjamin."

"Did he give you any trouble, Ollie?"

"That's putting it mildly. Took the entire night crew to subdue him."

"You know how the hospital feels about manhandling a patient," I said disapprovingly as I followed him down a narrow corridor.

"The boys were very scientific, Doctor. There's not a mark on him." He opened the barred cell. "Company, Pat."

Patrick O'Malley, a rotund man with a bristling red mustache and head of hair to match, was mummied to his ears in a white canvas strait-jacket. He looked up at me unhappily. "I was framed, Doc! So help me I was framed! There I was, down at Murphy's minding my own business, not bothering anybody, when they grabbed me."

"It says on your admission chart you were drunk, disorderly, profane, abusive and resisted arrest."

"All I had was three beers, Doc. Three lousy beers!"

I recoiled from his breath. "You're blowing off more than that now."

"Maybe it was four or five, but no hard stuff, Doc. Just beer."

"You know what Judge Elkins said he'd do if you showed up in his courtroom again?"

"You've got to help me, Doc," he pleaded. "I'll get six months, maybe a year! Can't you say I'm sick or something and get me transferred to the hospital?"

"The only way you could be moved out of here," I said, "would be for you to have a medical emergency like an acute appendix or a gall bladder."

"I knew you'd think of something, Doc. You're a genius."

"But you're not," I replied. "It's almost impossible to fake an acute abdomen. Besides I'm not on the surgical

service." I uncinched the leather straps on the strait-
jacket. His huge belly spilled out as I loosened the
canvas corset.

"Oh, that feels good," he sighed, vigorously scratch-
ing himself. "I don't see how my old lady stands that
armor plate of hers."

The sight of that enormous, pale white, hairless
abdomen gave me a wonderful idea. "If I get you out
of here, Pat . . ."

"I'll do anything you say, Doc."

"Anything, Pat?" I asked.

His bloodshot eyes looked at me warily. "Now wait a
minute. If you want someone worked over, O.K. But
I'm not bumping anyone off."

"It's nice to know you haven't lowered your stand-
ards, Pat. What I have in mind won't require any force,
just a little imagination."

Pat sat there fascinated while I briefly outlined my
scheme.

"I like being around you, Doc," he said admiringly.
"You make me feel like a saint."

"Now remember you can moan or groan, but you're
not to say a word. And if you start to laugh just cram
a towel in your mouth, understand?"

"I got you, Doc."

"If you muff this, Pat," I warned, "you're in here for
life!"

At one A.M. the following morning, Patrick O'Malley
was transferred to the hospital and admitted to a private room on the maternity service.

I briefed the obstetrical team on my plans. "I'm taking full responsibility for this delivery," I said to the

resident in charge. "You had nothing to do with this, understand?"

"I'm with you, Doctor," he said. "I'd give anything to see that cocky little devil on the receiving end for a change."

I turned to my volunteer helpers. "Now you all know what you're supposed to do?"

They grinned enthusiastically.

I put in an emergency call for Doctor Watson at the Navy Ball. Finally after a long period of waiting an irritated voice answered. "Hello, Henry," I shouted over the music. "This is Claude, Claude Benjamin. I'm sorry to be calling you at this hour, Henry, but I have an emergency here and I need your help."

"I never heard of a skin case being an emergency. Can't it wait till tomorrow?"

"This case is having a baby, Henry."

"A baby! How long has this been going on?"

"About nine months," I said.

"No, I don't mean that! Where are you now?"

"At the County Hospital."

"Isn't there someone there who can deliver the woman?"

"She insists on seeing you."

"How did she get my name?"

"I gave it to her, Henry. I said you were tops."

"You mean you called me away from the Ball just to tell me some charity case is having a lousy baby?"

"If that's how you feel about it, Henry," I said stiffly, "I'm sorry to have bothered you. It's just that the poor woman's blood pressure is over two hundred and she's having convulsions."

"Convulsions! Did you say convulsions?"

I held up a hand to silence my giggling audience. "That's what I said, Henry. If you're too busy, I guess I'll just have to turn her over to the resident physician. He hasn't had too much experience, but I'm sure he'll do his best. Have a nice time at the party."

"You keep that resident away from her, Claude. Do you hear? I'll be right over."

The stage was set. O'Malley's body had been draped so that his tremendous belly lay bare and his face was covered with a towel stained with mercurochrome. An interne was at the bedside taking his blood pressure.

Doctor Watson, young, very confident with a receding crewcut, made a dramatic entrance in his navy uniform. Betty followed him looking lovely in a dark green formal.

"I'm sorry to have spoiled your party, Henry," I said, avoiding Betty's eyes.

He waved me aside as he took a gown from the nurse. He turned gallantly to Betty. "Would you care to assist me, Miss Carstairs?"

"I'd love to, Doctor," she gushed. "I'll change and be right back."

Watson spotted the towel on O'Malley's face immediately.

"Bit her tongue," I explained.

"Where's her chart?" he asked.

"We didn't have time," I said, "her name is Miss Patricia O'Malley."

"Miss . . . ?" Watson stopped when he saw the student nurses standing in the room. "Now, Mrs. O'Malley," he began.

The belly rippled as O'Malley choked on his towel. "Another convulsion," I said.

"Blood pressure two hundred and thirty," murmured the interne.

Watson was not one to panic easily. He looked almost bored. "There, there, Madame." He solicitously patted O'Malley's arm. "We're going to be just fine."

O'Malley moaned through his towel.

Watson pushed me aside. "Let Miss Carstairs through, please. Now you stand right here, Betty."

"Thank you, Doctor," she said glaring at me.

Watson turned and smiled condescendingly at his growing audience. "I'm glad to see so many of you here," he said in his superior way. "It's not often you'll have the opportunity of observing my outlining technique." He took a blue crayon from his pocket. "I always find it helps to close your eyes while you visualize the baby's position." He closed his eyes as his fingers gently probed O'Malley. "The head's in the lower left quadrant," he murmured and made a mark with his crayon.

O'Malley groaned.

A look of annoyance crossed Watson's face. He closed his eyes again. "The shoulders should be here." Another mark with his crayon. "The back . . ." He opened his eyes. "An unusually large baby."

O'Malley choked and gargled through his towel.

"Please, Madame, you must be quiet!" Watson closed his eyes and resumed his examination. "What's this?" His fingers probed deeper. "Another head. Twins!" he cried excitedly. "Twins!"

A tidal wave swept down O'Malley almost knocking Watson to the floor.

"Fourteen," I said.

"Fourteen what?" Watson screamed over O'Malley's bellowing.

"Fourteen convulsions."

"Blood pressure two hundred and fifty," shouted the interne.

"Madame!" Watson's icy composure was beginning to fray at the edges. "You must learn to control yourself. Breathe through your mouth!" The huge belly threatened to explode. "Don't just stand there!" he shrieked at Betty. "Help me hold her." She held on gamely while the bed rocked and rolled. Slowly the quake subsided and once more the body lay still. Watson straightened up wearily.

"Can I be of any assistance, Doctor?" I asked solicitously.

"You keep away from me, Benjamin," he shrilled. "All the way away from me!"

I stepped back and looked sympathetically at Betty who was flushed and perspiring from her workout with O'Malley.

Watson took out his stethoscope and listened to the abdomen. A worried look crept into his eyes. "I can't hear the fetal heart tones," he complained. "Seems strange with all this motion there would be no heart tones." He turned viciously on Betty. "How do you expect me to hear over your deep breathing?"

"I'm sorry, Doctor, but I can't help it!" she said angrily.

"Hold your breath!" he glared at his audience. "Everyone hold their breath. I must have quiet!"

The room became very quiet.

"That's better." He tightened the stethoscope in his ears and listened again. "I hear it now," he cried triumphantly and made a mark with his crayon. "Here and there." He made another mark.

O'Malley choked and began to ripple again.

"Fifteen," I counted.

"Blood pressure two hundred and fifty," warned the interne.

Watson continued to listen. "The heart tones are becoming weaker. They're very weak." He pulled the stethoscope from his ears and turned frantically to Betty.

"Every minute counts! The babies' lives are at stake! Prepare for emergency surgery!"

"Yes, sir. Right away, sir."

O'Malley rose straight up in his bed. "Oh, no you don't!" he roared through his towel.

Watson forced him back to the mattress. "You must lie still, Madame. Think of your babies!"

O'Malley struggled free from Watson's grasp and tore the towel from his face. "To hell with the babies! I'm thinking of the mother!"

Watson's eyes dilated at the sight of that bristling red mustache and quietly collapsed in Betty's arms.

"Well, don't just stand there!" she said furiously to me. "Do something!"

"He's all yours," I said. "I'm sitting out this dance."

FROM *The Medical Itch*

Did I Ever Tell You About My Operation?
COREY FORD

Sometimes I wonder whose operation I had. Everybody shook hands with the doctor after it was over. People rushed up to congratulate the surgeon on his skill with the scalpel. There was nothing but praise for the anaesthetist. Tributes were paid to all the nurses and internes and technicians of the efficient hospital staff. Nobody had a word to say for me.

I don't want to sound ungrateful, but isn't it about time that somebody spoke up for the patient? I mean the pathetic little figure that the operation is all about. Everybody else is dressed in crisp white uniforms, but he is attired in an abbreviated nightshirt which barely comes down to the navel and is split all the way up the back, affording the wearer about as much protection as the paper filigree on the end of a lamb chop. His legs are encased in long woolen stockings, like the lower half of a bunny suit. He has a knitted skating cap on top of his head, with a name tag attached to the tassel so he won't get mixed up with some other patient and wind up in the maternity ward by mistake. No wonder that surgeons wear those gauze bandages over their faces. It's so the patient won't see them laughing.

It's his operation, but he has nothing to do with it. He cowers in his room, awaiting the ordeal that lies ahead. Nurses sneak up behind him without warning to take his temperature. Orderlies arrive at odd hours to shave him in even odder places. Surgeons halt beside his bed and study him with the appraising eye of a host about to carve a Thanksgiving turkey. He is thumped and squeezed and poked to see if he's tender. He is looked up and down and over and under and into. They listen to him with stethoscopes, they tap him with rubber hammers, they mark his epidermis here and there with a blue pencil. He can't ask them what's going on, because he has a thermometer in his mouth. All they ever tell him is "Hmm."

He doesn't even get to see the operation when it happens. Just about the time things start to get interesting, someone produces a hypodermic needle and says in a cheerful voice: "Roll over on your stomach." His limp form is wheeled into a shiny white room which bears an unpleasant resemblance to the metal meat counter under neon lights, as naked as Saturday's rib roast special, while two hundred medical students stare at him impersonally from the balcony. When he wakes up, he is back in his bed again with part of his anatomy swathed in bandages, a throbbing headache, and the uneasy conviction that sometime while he was coming out of the anaesthetic he asked the nurse's hand in marriage.

I speak with feeling, having served a stretch of time in a hospital myself. The whole affair, as I look back on it now, is a deliberate campaign to reduce the patient slowly but surely to a state of mental zero, in order to destroy his will to resist. From the moment I entered those big glass doors, I was subjected to a series of personal humiliations designed to undermine my pride and deflate my ego. Nobody can go through the daily rou-

tine of a hospital and have any dignity left. I defy even
General De Gaulle to look austere sitting on a bed-pan.

The brain-washing process started right off with my
accident. Actually it wasn't much of an accident. The
cause was a brief but violent argument between my car
and another car which tried to go where mine already
was. I am naturally a law-abiding citizen, and when
my car halted abruptly I obeyed the law of inertia and
kept on going until my progress was arrested by the
dashboard. As a result, the car was towed off to the
garage for repairs; I was towed off to the hospital.

I'm not sure what I expected to find when I got there.
Obviously I didn't really think the surgeon would be
waiting for me on the front steps, tight-lipped and
tense; but at least I had an idea that he might be
pacing up and down the corridor, chain-smoking and
glancing now and then out the window. I could picture
the look of relief on his face as the siren of my speeding
ambulance grew louder. "Not a moment to lose," I
could almost hear him shout, grinding his butt under a
heel as he sprang into action. "Light up the main operating room at once. Call Kildare and Casey in for consultation. This is undoubtedly the most unusual case
I've encountered in forty years of medical practice."

It didn't quite turn out that way. The ambulance
slowed down for every traffic light, and once it pulled
over to the curb while the driver went into a store to
buy some cigarettes. The only time he blew his siren
was when he stopped in front of the emergency entrance, evidently on the chance that some patient inside the hospital might be asleep. The orderly didn't

even look up as the ambulance attendant wheeled me in.

"Much of an accident?" he asked, placing a nine of hearts on his ten of spades and pushing back his chair reluctantly.

"Smashed the radiator, crumpled the left fender, and bent in the front axle a little," the attendant shrugged, as they slid me onto a table. "Tied up traffic for half an hour. Boy, was them other cars mad."

He wheeled the empty stretcher out, and the orderly began to take off my clothes. This is the first step when you enter a hospital. It doesn't matter whether you've come there to have a sliver removed from your finger, you have to get completely undressed. It's part of the whole insidious plot to degrade the patient, and is based on the theory that nobody can retain his self-respect when he has nothing on but a pair of black silk socks, with a hole in one toe.

The doctor seemed quite calm when he arrived twenty-five minutes later. In fact, if it hadn't been for my obviously critical condition, I might even have suspected that he was a little bored. He looked me over briefly, humming to himself, and whispered something to the nurse beside him. I braced myself for the worst.

"What's the verdict?" I asked in a grim let's-have-it-Doc-I-can-take-it tone.

"Now, there's nothing to worry about at all," he said in the soothing manner one might employ in addressing a slightly retarded child of six. "Humpty Dumpty had a bad fall, but we'll put him back together again snap! snap! in two shakes of a lamb's tail. The nurse will just give you a little shot, and you'll sleep like a baby."

You do everything else like a baby, too. Once the hospital gates clang behind you, you are as helpless as an infant in arms. To carry the idea out, your bed is covered with a rubber sheet and has slats on either side like a crib, to keep you from rolling onto the floor. The only thing lacking is an abacus and a set of plastic blocks. The nurse (it was all I could do to keep from calling her "Nannie") changes you when you're wet, feeds you through a straw, and pats you on the back to burp you afterwards. Your life is an open chart at the foot of your bed. Your most intimate functions are performed for all to see, and every move you make is eagerly recorded. There were times when I longed for the peace and quiet of an old-fashioned sanctuary behind the barn, hornets and all.

Your day starts at seven—the only institution that keeps worse hours than a hospital is the army—when the nurse tiptoes into your room to see if you're awake. We used to have a little game, Nannie and I. I would keep my eyelids shut while she bent over me, peering into my face intently. When I refused to stir, she would start moving around the room and making vague nurse-noises: squeaking her rubber soles on the linoleum, swishing her starched uniform against the edge of the bed, straightening invisible objects on the dresser, or taking the flowers out of their vases and snipping the stems one by one. If nothing else worked, she would drop an aluminum basin onto the floor with a resounding crash. This never failed to bring me bolt upright, whereupon she would inquire pleasantly: "Well, did we have a nice night's sleep?" (Nurses are also victims of we disease.) "Are we all ready for our bath?"

This daily ritual is always performed with a great show of modesty, as though you had any secrets from the nurse by now. First you are covered with a cotton blanket. While you clutch the upper hem desperately, to keep from skidding out of bed like a watermelon seed, all the rest of the bedclothes and your nightie are whisked out from under it, leaving you quivering raw. A tin tub filled with water is placed beside you, and just to keep pretenses up your limbs are withdrawn from beneath the protective coverlet one by one. Each section of your anatomy is washed and dried in turn, and discreetly put back under the blanket again before the next part is uncovered, so you won't all show at the same time. To make matters worse, my nurse's hands were invariably ice-cold—"Sign of a warm heart," she'd reassure me—and every time one of her frigid digits came in contact with my skin I would react violently, kicking out both legs and upsetting the bathtub.

Fortunately this didn't matter, because the bed-clothes had to be changed anyway. If there's one thing more humiliating than having the nurse give you a bath in bed, it's having your bed made while you are in it. In the first place, I never could figure out how she did it. I'd roll over onto one side, while a great deal of pulling and hauling would go on behind me. Then I would roll over onto the other side, crossing a sizeable ridge of bedding that seemed to have gathered at the small of my back, and the same yanking and tugging would begin all over again. By the time I rolled onto my back, the bed was all made, and here it was only seven-thirty.

The next problem is to find what to do with yourself all the rest of the day. You can wad your paper handkerchiefs into balls, and try to hit the wastebasket across the room. (Personally I developed an underhand lofting shot which could score two baskets out of three.) You can have an orderly crank the sections of your mechanical bed up and down, forming various geometric patterns or the more angular letters of the alphabet. It is possible to make a pretty good W, for example, by lowering the middle section and elevating the head and knees. Or else you can press the buzzer fastened to your pillow by a safety pin, and make book on how long it takes anybody to come.

If things get too dull, you can always play little jokes on your nurse, such as tipping over the water pitcher with an elbow, or falling out of bed. A friend of mine once livened up a long hospital day by smuggling a carton of live guppies into his room, and dumping them into his bedpan. The nurse screamed for the doctor, the doctor called the surgeon, and it was the end of the afternoon before things were settled down.

Then there are the fascinating little side trips to other parts of the hospital to have an X-ray picture taken or perhaps, if it's a red-letter day, to get a barium enema. These expeditions have all the elements of high adventure. You are loaded into a wheelchair and propelled down the corridor at a dizzy rate of speed, weaving in and out between patients on crutches and sideswiping an occasional service wagon filled with dishes. Doors open suddenly as you pass, or some other wheelchair comes hurtling around a corner, missing you by inches. You crowd into an elevator with three or four more patients all bound for the same destination, and the nurses discuss one another's cases in a detached professional way while the occupants glare at each other with frank loathing. I don't know where they get this theory that misery loves company. I hated every other patient on sight.

Your meals are served hospital-time, which means that dinner arrives about three in the afternoon, and has all the piquant flavor of a boiled head of steam. Usually a mimeographed menu is shown to you early in the morning, when you are full of energy, and you order a sizeable banquet including soup and dessert. By the end of the day your vitality has faded, and you lift the covers off the dishes one by one, and peer wanly at the china birdbaths filled with creamed carrots or mashed potatoes. It doesn't help when Nannie offers to cut up our chicken and feed us with a spoon.

Of course, a steady stream of people keep dropping into your room to help you while away the time. Next to a summer clearance sale, there's nothing like a "No Visitors" sign on the door to attract a crowd. Since your door is invariably left open, every passing stranger halts in the corridor and peers at you with morbid curiosity. Ambulatory patients in dressing growns wander in to sit beside your bed and show you pictures of their grandchildren. If you happen to doze off during the afternoon, the nurse wakes you up to give you another sleeping tablet.

The hospital staff goes out of its way to keep you from getting lonely. There's the cleaning woman, for instance, who arrives in the middle of breakfast and proceeds to mop the floor with some pine-smelling disinfectant, lending a slight taste of turpentine to your coffee. There's the daily visit of the young lady who comes to get another sample of your blood. She carries a tray of bottles hung from her neck, like a cigarette girl in a nightclub, and beams with anticipation as she selects a particularly long needle and inquires: "Let's see, which side did we do yesterday?" I used to shut my eyes whenever I saw her coming, but I have an impression that she had pointed teeth and hung upside down from the ceiling.

And then there's the newsstand lady who brings you the morning paper, along with the latest gossip about your neighbors down the hall. "Number Fourteen had another relapse last night, they got her under oxygen, it probably won't be long now." "I see where the bed in Twenty-Eight is empty, I guess that means one less *Herald-Tribune* for this floor." Or, even more ominously: "I hope I have better luck with your room than the last three times."

Last but not least, there are the acquaintances who drop around to cheer you up. You can hear them coming all the way down the corridor, laughing boisterously at some private joke as they approach your door. They all have deep tans and are fairly bursting with health as they storm into your room and greet you with hearty humor. "Look at you, boy, you sure seem to be taking it easy." "Wish I had nothing else to do but loaf in bed all day." They make themselves right at home, tossing a hat onto your dresser and knocking over a vase of tulips, or selecting an apple from your fruit basket and biting into it with a loud crunch. "Do you mind if I smoke?" one of them asks, lighting a cigar and blowing a cloud of heavy fumes into your face. Another rummages through the books on the table. "Say, here's one I never read," he remarks idly, slipping a half-finished detective novel into his pocket. Another slides everything off your bedside stand and sits on it, propping his feet on the edge of your mattress while he regales you with all the fun they've been having lately.

"Sure wish you coulda been along last night," he recalls, crossing his legs and upsetting the ashtray onto your pillow. "We wound up at three in the morning, I took out that little blonde you used to date before the accident, she told me to be sure 'n say hello."

At least, these visits never last very long. "I'm afraid we gotta be going," someone announces suddenly, and all the others spring to their feet with obvious relief. "We're all driving out to the country this weekend for a real blast." He hesitates beside your bed. "By the way, is it okay if we borrow the keys to your car? You probably won't be needing it for a while."

The room is very quiet after they've gone. The air is blue with smoke, the floor is littered with apple cores and cigar butts, and water drips steadily from the overturned vase on the dresser. You reach for the buzzer to call the nurse, but someone has accidentally kicked the plug out of the socket. You lean back on your ash-covered pillow, and close your eyes.

Comes the long-awaited day when baby attempts his first faltering steps. You sit on the edge of the bed, while the nurse fits a pair of slippers onto your dangling feet and works your arms backward into a bathrobe. Taking a deep breath, you lower your legs to the floor and stand erect. You are surprised to discover how far away the floor is. Your head seems to be floating in space, and you expect to feel it bump along the ceiling like a toy balloon. Nannie holds your arm to steady you, and whispers encouragingly: "Just take it easy, first our left foot in front of us, and then our right one, *that's* the way."

You reject her assistance with a superior smile. After all, you're a big grown-up man now. You can walk by yourself without help. Why, you're doing fine. How about strolling over and glancing into the bathroom? You've been paying for a private bath, you might as well see what it looks like. You get as far as the door-jamb and grab it suddenly, because the room has started spinning around like a revolving door and there are at least half a dozen blurred Nannies in front of you. It takes all six of them to get you back across the room to your bed again.

The days whiz by like glaciers, and you are ready to be discharged from the hospital at last. It takes you most of the afternoon to pack. You arrived with a small overnight bag, but the get-well cards and empty vases and fruit baskets you have accumulated during your illness now fill three suitcases and a large cardboard carton. You dress yourself slowly, taking a good long rest after donning each successive garment, and let Nannie help you lace your shoes. The neckband of your shirt feels as big as a horse collar, and your suit hangs so loosely from your emaciated frame that you glance furtively at the label to see if by any chance it belongs to somebody else. Leaning on a cane, you proceed down the hall, smiling at the less fortunate patients as you pass their doors. "Goodbye, Mrs. Hostetter, hope you'll be getting out soon." "Look out for that blonde nurse of yours, Mr. Freem." You wave a sentimental farewell to all the orderlies and dieticians and student nurses who have been so nice to you, trying to conceal the fervid hope that you'll never see any of their leering faces again, and descend in the elevator to the main floor and totter across the lobby to the street.

So this is that fresh air that everybody else has been breathing all this time. Look at those flowers growing right in the ground, not in a glass receptacle. Look at all those pretty girls in spike-heel pumps instead of sensible white shoes with corrugated rubber soles. Your hospital stretch is over. You're a free man now. All you need is a warden to shake your hand and give you an envelope with ten dollars.

Your apartment looks exactly as it did when you left it that fatal morning. Nothing has changed in your bedroom. Your brush and comb are still on the dresser, your pajamas are still hanging on the floor of the closet, the cap is still off the toothpaste tube, the magazine you were reading is still lying open on the bedside table beside a pack of stale cigarettes. The whole thing has a musty smell, like George Washington's bedroom at Mount Vernon. The only thing missing is an attendant in a mobcap and a velvet rope across the door. Your desk is piled high with mail, but you're too tired to look at it now. A glass of fruit juice would certainly taste good, but there's no buzzer to press for Nannie. Nobody to give you a back rub, you reflect ruefully.

Nobody to tuck you into bed tonight, nobody to bring your supper on a tray, nobody to wake you tomorrow morning and ask you if we had a good night's sleep and how would we like our bath?

At least, you comfort yourself, all your friends will be waiting impatiently to hear all about your hospital experience. This illusion is promptly shattered. I've been trying to tell people about my operation ever since I had it, but I can't find anybody to listen. It's getting so that everybody avoids me at parties, and acquaintances cross the street when they see me coming.

That's why I hurried over here to the hospital to see you, as soon as I heard about this operation of yours. Do you mind if I close the door of your room to make sure nobody disturbs us? I'll just sit on the edge of your bed, so you can't wriggle out from under the covers and get away. Maybe I'd better disconnect this buzzer in case you want to ring for the nurse.

Now, then. Let me tell you what happened to *me*.

FROM *And How Do We Feel This Morning?*

Operation Operation

JEAN KERR

Obviously this is not the moment to be talking about operations when here we all are—in the very bloom of health. But these are troubled times, and there are people in St. Vincent's Hospital today who, as recently as yesterday, didn't know they *had* a spinal disk. The thing to do, I say, is be prepared, bone up, get the facts so that your stay in the hospital will be the jolly, satisfying interlude it ought to be.

I don't know whether or not I am speaking for convalescents everywhere, but I can tell you that *my* big mistake when I go to the hospital is being too cheerful. I arrive the day before the operation and, while it would be stretching things to suggest that on this occasion I feel fit, I at least feel human. So I try to be agreeable. Agreeable nothing; I'm adorable to a point just short of nausea. With my gay sayings and my air of quiet self-deprecation, I creep into the heart of one and all.

"Yes," I murmur to the night nurse, "I did ring for you an hour ago, but that's *perfectly* all right." And I reassure the orderly who forgot to bring my dinner tray with a blithe "Don't worry about it, I'm not the least bit hungry and besides I have these delicious cherry cough drops."

But then the morrow comes, and with it my operation. As I'm wheeled back from the Recovery Room it becomes absolutely clear that, while the operation was a great success, I am a total failure. I feel completely, utterly, unspeakably miserable, and I see no reason why any member of the staff should be kept in ignorance of this sorry state of affairs. I ring bells, buzz buzzers, snap at nurses, and generally behave in a manner that can best be described as loathsome.

Of course, the nurses have seen post-operative cases before, but clearly they expected more of *me*. It's as though June Allyson had been transformed into Ana Pauker right before their eyes. And they feel, not unreasonably, that they have been betrayed. As a result, the whole staff gives me approximately the same brisk, gingerly attention they would bestow on an old bandage. Even at the end of the fourth day—when I'm once again feeling pro-social and want to kiss and make up—they will have none of me.

The best solution to this problem, short of being a good little soldier all the time, is to be a teensy bit curt when you first arrive. Don't pose as an Eva Marie Saint. Show your true colors. Keep your tone brisk. Then there will be no unpleasant shocks later.

And there are other steps you can take. Actually, to cope with ordinary hospital routine you really ought to be in good physical condition. Since this is hardly practical—you wouldn't be in the hospital if you were in good physical condition—you can do the next best thing: be mentally alert, be systematic. Remember: if they have rules, *you* have rules.

Rule One: *Refuse to be bullied.* It is the custom in most hospitals for the night nurse to wake all her patients before she goes off duty at six o'clock in the morning and present each of them with a basin of luke-warm water and a bar of soap. Then, a few seconds later, the incoming day nurse rushes in and takes everybody's temperature. This is a very sensible procedure because most people say they notice a very definite rise in temperature (together with a tendency to break down and sob) merely at being required to *look* at a basin of water at six o'clock in the morning, and the day nurse now has something concrete to put on her chart. She doesn't have to feel a failure.

How do you eliminate this dawn patrol? It's no use complaining to the nurse; she's met your type before. Any piteous explanations on your part like, "Nurse, please, I haven't been to sleep at all, they just gave me a sedative half an hour ago and besides I'm clean, look, *clean!*" will only confirm her growing suspicion that you have no team spirit and, what's worse, no regard at all for personal daintiness.

After much trial and error I have worked out a rather neat little system for beating this game. I simply explain to the nurse that I am undergoing psychoanalysis for an old guilt trauma which dates back to the time when I was three years old and shoved my little sister into a golf bag. Ever since, I tell her, I've shown manifestations of the Lady Macbeth complex, an aberration in which the victim has a continuous and compulsive desire to wash her hands. Consequently, as a part of my therapy I am forbidden by my analyst to wash more than three times a day.

I am also working on a plan—it's unfortunately still in the blueprint stage—that would limit the number of times a nurse took your temperature to something reasonable, say eight or nine times in a single afternoon. At that, it's not really the frequency that's so maddening, it's the duration. What do you suppose there is in the Nightingale code that impels a nurse to put a thermometer in somebody's mouth just before she goes off to assist at an appendectomy? There you are, left like a beached submarine with this little periscope poking from your mouth while all about you life goes on, children are born, and you who have so much to contribute can do nothing but nibble on that damn little glass tube.

I just take it out the minute her back is turned and carefully replace it about five minutes before she returns. There's no real risk of detection, because a truly conscientious nurse will always stop off at the linen closet on her way back and her approach will be heralded by the snatches of fascinating dialogue that float down the corridors:

"Listen, fourteen needs a top sheet."

"Nonsense, I gave fourteen two sheets yesterday."

"Okay, you tell that to fourteen."

The system is practically foolproof.

Rule Two: *Act your age*. One of the most difficult things to contend with in a hospital is the assumption on the part of the staff that because you have lost your gall bladder you have also lost your mind. Personally, I find it rather piquant to be treated like a four-year-old. ("Are we feeling any better? Shall we sit up and eat our nice lunch?") The only objectionable aspect of this constant use of the plural is that it leaves me with the feeling that I'm *two* four-year-olds.

And you do have to say one thing for these cuddly, nursy-knows-best disciplinarians: they're loyal, they complete the task assigned. Neither storm nor sleet nor gloom of night will stay them from the swift completion of their appointed rounds. This was brought home to me in a very real way during my last sojourn in the hospital when a dear little night nurse woke me up from a sound sleep to give me a sleeping pill. Sometimes this business of hewing to the narrow line of duty produces results bordering on the miraculous. A writer I once heard about flew to Evanston to visit his eighty-year-old mother who had just had an operation. Arriving, he met a nurse in the corridor, asked for a report on the patient, and was told that she had made all the routine objections to being put on her feet five days after the operation but that the staff had been firm, quite firm, and now the old lady was trotting around like everybody else. The writer was deeply impressed. "Good Lord," he said, "she hasn't walked in five years."

You see the point, don't you? If the lady in question had stood on her rights as an eighty-year-old, she'd still be sitting pretty in that rocking chair, where she wanted to be.

Rule Three: *Get the facts.* It seems to me that too many people accept hospital routine with cowlike apathy, whereas a little intellectual curiosity would be broadening to the patient and stimulating to the staff. Let's say that two interns approach you with a cartful of sinister-looking tubes and announce casually, "We're going to give you a Harris Flush."

Don't just lie there. Get the whole story. Who was Harris? What is this flush? When did Harris get the idea in the first place? Whatever happened to Harris?

Why shouldn't you ask a question from time to time? It's only quid pro quo. From the moment you get into that hospital coat and they lock away your shoes, there is a constant parade of cheery interns, all of them popping with more questions than Mary Margaret McBride. What was your mother's maiden name? Did you ever have any broken limbs? How old were you when

you had chicken pox? If there is anything more strik-
ing than their fascination with that attack of measles
you had in 1927, it's their total disinterest in that rup-
tured appendix which explains your presence here at
this moment.

My father spent some time in a hospital a couple of
years ago, and he began by being very patient and
co-operative about answering all the routine questions.
At the end of an hour's inquisition the intern asked
him how old *his* father was when he died. Dad explained, with pardonable pride, that his father had died
at the age of ninety-five. The intern looked up from
his notes and inquired, with the air of one about to
make a significant discovery, "What did he die of?"
Whereupon my father exploded. "My God, man, he
died because he was *ninety-five!*"

While interns may be lacking in other qualities, I
want no one to tell me that they don't have a sense of
humor. At first glance, this sense of humor may seem a
trifle macabre. Actually, it fits perfectly into the cold,
brilliant tradition of Ben Jonson, Dean Swift, and
Charles Addams. Why else would an intern deposit a
patient due for an eight-o'clock operation outside the
operating-room door at seven-thirty, where she will be
in a position to overhear the highlights of the preced-
ing operation?

You can picture the scene, can't you? There is the patient, strapped to a cart, partially sedated, and feeling
a good deal less than hearty. And through the transom
comes a rough male voice saying, "Boy, I never thought
it would spurt like *that*." Oh, there's no end to the pos-
sibilities for good, clean, sinister mirth.

Rule Four: *Look the part.* Let's not pretend that all the mistakes made in hospitals are made by the staff. I've known patients who have made beauts. As far as I'm concerned, there is nothing more idiotic than the spectacle of a woman just coming out of ether who immediately struggles into a fluffy pink bed jacket and ties a tender blue ribbon into her limp curls. Though scarcely able to lift an arm, she somehow succeeds in applying two layers of make-up before the stroke of visiting hour.

What happens? Gay husband arrives, bearing an azalea, and announces, "Boy, honey, *you* look great, but let me tell you about the day I had!"

My own theory, which owes something—at least in spirit—to T. S. Eliot's principle of the "objective correlative," can be stated simply: if you feel terrible, look terrible. Save that blue ribbon until the happy moment arrives when you notice that you can comb even the back of your hair without becoming so faint that you have to lie down for half an hour afterwards. In addition to the fact that by simulating recovery you get none of the sympathy which psychologists tell us is so necessary in convalescence, you run the further risk of being brought home from the hospital prematurely. There you'll be, back in the kitchen frying pork chops, when everybody knows you need rest, rest, rest. So I say: no lipstick, forget about the cold cream, *let* those fine lines appear. Make it very difficult for your friends to tell you that they never saw you looking better in your life. With any luck, you may even startle an acquaintance into making an intelligent remark, like

"Helen, you poor darling, you look ghastly—I bet you feel rotten, don't you?"

Rule Five: I'm sorry, but Rule Five seems to have gone out of my head. I have this sharp pain. Well, it's more like a twinge than a pain—but a *deep* twinge. Excuse me while I call Dr. Meredith.

FROM *Please Don't Eat the Daisies*

CHAPTER IV

The Blessed Event

Just as each hospital generally has a separate ward for maternity patients, so too does that class of hospital happening called "the baby" deserve a place of its own in this anthology. The authors of each of this chapter's selections are eminently qualified to write on their subjects. Kenneth Morgan, who discusses the various types of expectant mothers, is a practicing obstetrician, and Frank Gilbreth, Jr., who dissertates on the paternal aspects of childbirth, is himself a father. Both approach their subject matter from a new angle— namely that of humor, for there are no funnier participants in the divine comedy than the mother and the father.

Heroine

KENNETH R. MORGAN, M.D.

In characterizing the heroine there is no risk of dogmatism. No two pregnant women are precisely the same—nor two non-pregnant women for that matter. When you come right down to it, no *one* woman is the same from one day to the next. Of course, I'm writing as a male. Females claim to find nothing enigmatic in each other. But even as a male Gynecologist who sees nothing but women all day every day, and who is presumed therefore to understand them, I find myself frequently thrown off balance.

Why, for example, does stolid, phlegmatic Mrs. Schultz, who has never done more than grunt laconically when you speak to her, suddenly burst into tears and launch into a tirade against the human race just because you tell her the X-ray shows twins? What's wrong with twins? So, supposing she does have six children at home and got pregnant this time by accident? Is that any reason to howl and yell and claim all husbands are rats? I guess so. Twins have apparently gone out of style, poor things.

Or, as another example, how about Mrs. Gizmo who spends nine months regarding you with venomous distaste; and then, on coming out of anesthesia and being told she has a boy, grabs you around the neck and kisses you full on the mouth. (The fact that she vomits immediately thereafter I prefer to attribute to the ether.)

All one can say, where women are concerned, is that life is a succession of surprises. Still, there are certain categories in which they can be placed, at least tentatively.

1. Troubled Waters

This girl comes into your office holding little pieces of shredded Kleenex. The eyes roll. Cascades of perspiration exude from every pore. Her mother says the experience is frightful. Her grandmother said it was awful beyond belief. You can try to assure her it can't be all that bad or nobody would ever have more than one child. No dice. We'll go bravely to the electric chair. After the birth is over and we find ourselves relatively unhurt, terror is replaced by delight. These people make very satisfactory patients for the Obstetrician. Whatever happens it's better than they expected.

2. Unruffled Feathers

This is the opposite side of the coin. Nothing bothers us. Pregnancy is something to be ignored. We take ballet; we ride motorcycles; we build stone walls. After it's over we breast-feed while water-skiing. These girls are almost always ex-captains of a Field Hockey team, and can be spotted a mile away by the short cropped hair, the stretch pants, and the sandals. I have nothing but admiration for them. They make Pocahontas look like Cleopatra.

3. Brood Mare

Here we have a girl without a saturation point. When you ask her when her last period was she scratches her head and says, "I think maybe it was 1946." The peculiar characteristic of the constant mother is an apparent unawareness of offspring. She brings all twelve children into the office and sits indifferently by while they tear up the magazines, crayon the walls, and grind lollypops into the rug. Some protective mechanism has long since deafened her to the sound of her wee ones in fighting trim. She responds only to distress signals—never to those exultant cries indicative of vandalism.

Aside from the repair bills, the Obstetrician has no complaint with these dedicated individuals. They invariably propel the newborn infant into his waiting hands after a twenty-minute labor: and return faithfully, year after year after year.

4. Thursday's Child

It's my observation that the young married girl in her first pregnancy is getting younger every year—whether through free choice or out of respect for the parental shot gun is equivocal. The teen-age mothers always appear with a face full of chewing gum and giggle merrily at each medical question. They all share the common quality of being ticklish. Lay a hand on them and they double up and give vent to high pitched squeals. At first the Obstetrician finds the whole bit somewhat unnerving. But eventually he gets into the swing of things and finds himself entering the examining room snapping his fingers and singing, "Ya! Ya! Ya!" —anything for the sake of *rapport*.

5. Femme Fatale

Occasionally one encounters a girl dedicated to scuttling the doctor-patient relationship. She wants things to be *intime*. She asks questions like, "How can you get excited about making love to your wife, doing what *you* do all day?" or, "Suppose you get a call when you're snoggered on too many Martinis?"

I may be wrong, but I have a feeling that these girls are not really intent on a flirtation. I'm sure if a man were to suggest a motel they'd flee his presence with the speed of light. I think they're motivated by a resentment of a doctor's paternal attitude, and yearn to cut him down to size.

I see no reason to fight this. In answer to the first question I would say, "Oh, but my wife is different from other women. She has three of everything!" To the second query the logical reply would be, "I never drink Martinis. I only get snoggered on Bourbon." With a little ingenuity one can parry almost any type of personal remark.

6. Jubilee

The pleasantest type of heroine is the one who considers the entire business of child-bearing a complete lark. Everything is too wonderful for words. Heartburn is wonderful, nose bleeds are wonderful, even hemorrhoids are wonderful.

The only hazard is that, should she fall down and

break a leg, she might also consider that to be wonderful. You have to warn these girls to be sure and
report such trivia as broken bones, massive arterial
hemorrhages, or sudden unexplained paralyses.

7. Oh Dear, What Can the Matter Be?

The above heroine is counterbalanced by Madam
Morbidity who fears that each hour is certain to be her
last on earth. Her entire pregnancy is spent on the
phone talking to doctors, relatives, friends, and strangers on the party line—anybody who will reassure her
that a pimple on the neck doesn't necessarily mean that
the baby will be stillborn.

During labor she cheers up everybody in attendance
by asking, "Will I make it?" at two minute intervals.
Sometimes she varies the enquiry by asking, "Isn't it
time to call for the priest?"

8. Time Study

An occasional heroine inhabits a world of her own—
a world inhabited only by people anxious for her happiness and comfort. She comes to her Obstetrician's office bearing a stenographer's pad, a carton of cigarettes,
and a box lunch. Once in his presence she settles down
for a nice two hour chat, oblivious to the thirty-five
people in the waiting room—some standing, some sitting on radiators, some hanging from the chandeliers.
The stenographer's pad is completely filled with notes,
often listed in alphabetical order, viz:

Adam's Apple: Should it rise and fall when a person
    swallows?
Burp: Must I?

Constipated: Why aren't I?

Decisions: I can't make any.

Embarrassments: I dreamt I outgrew my Maidenform Bra.

Figure: Will I ever get it back?

Ghastly: Is it necessary to feel this way?

Housework: Best to abstain, yes?

And so it goes, all the way to Z. There is no way of turning this off other than opening a window and jumping out.

9. Dollar Value

This girl is the descendant of a long line of pennywise ancestors. She knows that the price of her delivery includes certain ancillary services, such as unlimited telephone consultations and extra office visits. It's foolish not to take advantage of these fringe benefits.

She calls on Christmas Eve to ask if you can recommend a veterinarian for her sister's poodle. She persuades you to open up the office Easter Sunday so she can show you her new stretch mark. There's nothing vindictive here. She's been brought up in a philosophy of getting the most for one's dollar. So, why not?

Perhaps the Obstetrician should be sporting about it and play the same game. This could be done by adding $50 to the bill for "extras"—let's say $20 for reading the magazines in the waiting room, $15 for wear and tear on the upholstery, $10 for use of the elevator, and $5 for paper towels. I'm afraid it would never work.

10. In Absentia

Some heroines have long since departed Cloud 9 and gone on to Cloud 97. With luck they may keep one appointment out of five. If they do it's only because the receptionist has contacted them just as they were going out the door on their way to the movies. Every now and then they surprise you by showing up unexpectedly. Their appointment with you has been confused with an appointment at the hairdresser's. On the rare occasions when they appear on the correct day it is always at the incorrect hour.

I can't get too indignant about this. Patients often wait for doctors; and turn-about is fair play. Still, it would be nice if they didn't show up just as you were in the midst of a worrisome interview with the Internal Revenue Service.

11. Poker Face

I realize that in the description of obstetrical heroines I am simply describing people. These are the same girls who behave in the same way whether in a doctor's office or a supermarket. I suppose the most unrewarding of all types is the Non-give. You break your neck unrolling the red carpet and she kicks it aside. Time the roast beef just right and she'll be late for dinner. The Obstetrician says, "Look, dearie, you have nothing to worry about." And she answers, "I should hope not. That's what I'm paying you for."

Confronted with such a glacial wall, young and inexperienced Obstetricians run around chasing their tails and begging to be allowed to run after a stick. Old and experienced ones sit back on their haunches and say, "Look, dearie, you have nothing to worry about except your own miserable personality. How would you like to drop dead?" Oddly enough, this is usually interpreted as an endearing remark.

12. Horrible Heffalump

We come finally to the girl who is not at all pleased with being pregnant. This is obvious whenever you ask her anything.

"Do your ankles swell?"

"My God, *do* they—like balloons!"

"Do you sleep well?"

"Sleep! I haven't slept five minutes in the past six months!"

Confronted with this sort of heroine the experienced Obstetrician loads his questions.

"Have you noticed any purple spots behind your knees?"

"Purple! *Puce* would be more like it!"

"Do you hear little bells ringing when you close your eyes?"

"Little bells! Talk about Chinese gongs and you'll be nearer the truth!"

"Ah," you say to yourself. "This is a heroine worthy of my mettle." When she sends you a picture of the baby the following Christmas together with a note of thanks, you know you've accomplished something—even though it may have sapped your last ounce of resilience.

I know that there are other categories such as the fastidious heroine, the frowzy heroine, and the positively unsanitary heroine. I also realize that categories overlap and heroines often fall into more than one.

Try to pin them down and you find yourself out on a limb. That's womankind for you. No matter what—the heroine is sure to have the last laugh.

FROM *A Little Stork Told Me*

Little Monster
FRANK B. GILBRETH, JR.

New babies bear little resemblance whatsoever to anything living, and to not very many things that are dead.

What they *really* look like is the drawings in the maternity books of horrid little tadpoles, bent over into circles inside the mothers.

The father should try to keep all of this in mind, as he walks from the waiting room to his wife's room.

The first thing he wants to know, of course, is how his wife is feeling. He's immensely relieved to find that, instead of looking haggard and tortured as he had feared, she looks rested and wonderful.

And then he sees the baby! No matter how well prepared the father may be, this first glimpse of his newborn flesh and blood is apt to be a disheartening experience. His initial thought is that the squalling, naked little creature is embarrassingly premature—not ready yet, by a long shot, to be exposed to the human eye.

The father's natural inclination, when thus confronted by what appears to be one of nature's ghastly secrets, is to avert his gaze and decently turn away his head. He may even wonder whether it will be at all possible to send the baby back where it came from for further incubation and development.

Of course the father will realize almost instantly that any such return is out of the question and therefore amounts to no more than wishful thinking.

He then may steal a look at the nurse and another look at his wife, expecting to find them ready to burst into tears. Certainly, he thinks, he has every right to expect sympathy and commiseration, before the pathetic little thing is mercifully covered with a sheet and hustled over to the medical college or the zoo or someplace for observation.

It is at this point that the mother can be expected to remark happily to her husband, "The baby looks just like you, dear."

It is extremely important for the husband to control himself when this damaging statement comes pouring from the lips of his mate.

He must do his level best to remember that, while he was going through his miserable ordeal in the waiting room, she was not having an easy time of it in the delivery room, either. Consequently, she cannot yet be held entirely responsible for her remarks, however insulting they may sound. Surely it will be a very bad mistake indeed for the husband to lose his temper and snap back that there are no monkeys, tadpoles, or sideshow freaks on *his* side of the family.

Instead, he should be prepared to respond, in as pleasant a tone as possible, somewhat along this line:

"Why, you flatterer, you! Really, dear, the precious little thing looks just like *you*."

Then if the father is properly observant, he will notice that, far from being on the brink of tears, the mother and the nurse are both beaming, and obviously expect him to do the same.

For the benefit of those prospective fathers who otherwise might have trouble beaming, it may be helpful for me to describe in detail here the exact appearance of the average new baby. What does the helpless, grotesque, diminutive creature really look like?

Tiny—unbelievably tiny. In fact so tiny that it must be seen to be thoroughly dreaded. Red, swollen, mottled, angry, and almost utterly bald. Lopsided head. Puffy eyes sealed shut like those of a beaten prize fighter. A flat, shapeless nose. Toothless gums which give an old man's look to a collapsible and disappearing chin. No neck worth mentioning. A withered pumpkin stem for a navel. Scaly and almost white hands and feet, to which circulation seems to be coming belatedly. Nails that need cutting. A pathetic, reedy, nagging voice employed in anger, hunger, and discomfort.

I suggested earlier that it is a good idea for the husband to start paying surreptitious visits to the maternity floor of the hospital, long before his own baby is born. The purpose of such visits now becomes clear. For if the husband has studied and observed, through the plate-glass window of the nursery, the physical characteristics of infants in general, he will not be so thoroughly demoralized by the appearance of his own child.

To be sure, none of the infants observed on such visits will be quite as new-born and frightening as the

husband's *own* baby. And for that reason, some fathers
have been known to faint at the first sight of babies,
despite numerous advance visits to the nursery. Indeed,
some fathers of large families—who have already been
through the ordeal a great many times and should be
familiar with what to expect—*still* occasionally blanch
and faint at the first shocking sight. Just the same, in
most cases the advance visits to the nursery are helpful.
It should be remembered, too, that fainting is the exception, not the rule.

The new mother is, of course, instantly and immensely proud of the baby. And whether or not this
pride is contagious, the new father will find to his surprise that his initial shame is fleeting. In fact, by the
time his baby is placed on display with the others in
the nursery, the shame is so completely forgotten that
the father is apt to deny, even to himself, that it ever
existed. And in its place is a chest-swelling pride, a
monumental pride, surpassing even that of the mother.

The symptom of this monumental pride is a silly,
vacant grin, displayed as the father stands entranced,
watching his offspring through the nursery window.

His baby is still bald, toothless, neckless, red, mottled, and swollen. But for some reason, the father now
thinks that, instead of being a ghastly mistake of nature, the little thing is sublimely perfect, a Dresden
china miniature of himself.

Within a matter of hours, the new father becomes a
garrulous expert on babies' weights. A few days before,
he couldn't have said whether an average baby weighs
two pounds or twenty-two pounds. Now he knows to
the ounce not only what his own infant weighed at

birth, but what most of the other babies in the nursery weighed as well.

Needless to say, he is convinced that *his* baby's weight is ideal. If the child is big and heavy, the father congratulates himself on his virility and never loses an opportunity to patronize the fathers of smaller infants. On the other hand, if his child is petite, he congratulates himself for not having an old cow of a wife, and he strongly implies to other fathers that their offsprings are gross and bloated.

Through the nursery window the father discovers a number of extremely attractive and unusual things about the baby that had been previously overlooked— perhaps a wisp of hair at the very top of the otherwise nude skull, a dimple on the elbow, well-developed arm muscles, a heart-shaped chin, a cupid's bow on the upper lip, a high and intelligent forehead, sturdy legs.

Of course there is a fairly good chance that the father is looking at the wrong baby—but no matter. By the time the poor soul comes down to earth again, he'll never realize his mistake.

At this stage, the father is such a pathetically vulnerable creature, so nakedly unprotected in his inflated pride, that nurses he has never seen before, nice old ladies, and other kind-hearted utter strangers will take pity on him.

"Which one is *yours?*" they will ask, as he stands mesmerized in front of the nursery window. And then, when he points vacantly at the particular little creature which for the moment he thinks is his, they will add kindly, perhaps exchanging a wink with a friend as they do so:

"My, not *that* one. Why, that's the one everyone's raving about. Isn't that child a beauty? Goodness, how proud you must be!"

A few hours before, the father would have been inclined to summon the man with the butterfly net for anyone who described that tadpole as a "beauty." A few days before, he would have been suspicious and felt for his wallet on hearing such extravagant praise.

But now, it never even occurs to him that he is being gently teased, or that the compliment is not richly deserved. In fact the compliment only serves to confirm his own impression. And he is convinced that the remark has sprung naturally and spontaneously from the lips of an impartial stranger, on beholding a wondrous sight.

FROM *How to Be a Father*

CHAPTER V

Do It Yourself,
If You Dare

The professional healer has a long history, but even he is antedated by the do-it-yourself seeker of health. Even today, millions of people will try anything from store-bought drugs to age-old folk elixirs before they reluctantly visit a doctor. Most of the ills thus treated are, of course, minor ones. One transient affliction in particular usually incites so many well-intended suggestions that the suffering patient only succeeds in adding bewilderment to his plight. The name of this dread malaise is hiccoughs. A typical experience with hiccoughs is hilariously chronicled by the master humorist, Robert Benchley.

Running a close second to hiccoughs in the number of "sure" cures is insomnia. To those suffering from insomnia, my numbering all of the various remedies would be both unnecessary and cruel. But Saul Jarcho has come up with a novel treatment that utilizes one of the oldest known sleep-inducing agents known to man: boredom.

Stop Those Hiccoughs!

ROBERT BENCHLEY

Anyone will be glad to admit that he knows nothing about beagling, or the Chinese stock market, or ballistics, but there is not a man or woman alive who does not claim to know how to cure hiccoughs. The funny thing is that the hiccoughs are never cured until they get darned good and ready.

The most modest and unassuming man in the world becomes an arrogant know-it-all in the presence of hiccoughs—in somebody else.

"Don't be silly," he says, patronizingly. "Just put your head under your arm, hold a glass of water against the back of your neck, and count to five hundred by fives without taking a breath. It never fails."

Then, when it *has* failed, he blames you. "It's absolutely surefire if you only follow my directions," he says. He also implies darkly that what is ailing you is not just merely hiccoughs. "My method can't be expected to cure drunkenness, you know," he says.

To date, I have been advised to perform the following feats to cure hiccoughs:

Bend the body backward until the head touches the floor, and whistle in reverse.

Place the head in a pail of water and inhale twelve times deeply.

Drink a glass of milk from the right hand with the right arm twisted around the neck until the milk enters the mouth from the left side.

Hop, with the feet together, up and down a flight of steps ten times, screaming loudly at each hop.

Roll down a long, inclined lawn, snatching a mouthful of grass up each time the face is downward.

I have tried them all, with resultant torn ligaments, incipient drowning, lockjaw and arsenic poisoning, but, each time, at the finish of the act, and a few seconds of waiting while my mentor says, triumphantly: "See! What did I tell you?" that one, big hiccough always breaks the tension, indicating that the whole performance has been a ghastly flop.

My latest fiasco came as the result of reading the prescription of a Boston doctor, and almost resulted in my being put away as an irresponsible person. "All that the sufferer has to do," wrote the doctor, "is to blow up an ordinary paper bag, as if to explode it and then hold it over the mouth and nose tightly, breathing in and out of the bag instead of in and out of the open air."

This, according to the doctor, creates an excess of carbon monoxide gas in the bag, which is breathed over and over again, acting on a nervous center of the brain and curing the hiccoughs.

Being alone in the room at the time, I blew the bag up and held it tightly over my face, including not only my mouth and nose, but my eyes as well, like a gas-mask. I subjected myself to this treatment for possibly three minutes, walking around the room at the same time to keep from getting bored.

When I removed the bag I found myself the object of the silent but terrified scrutiny of my wife, who had entered the room without my knowing it, and who had already motioned for corroborating witnesses from the next room, two of whom were standing in the doorway, transfixed.

My explanation that I was curing hiccoughs did not go very big, as what I had obviously been doing was walking around the room alone with a paper bag over my head. This is *not* a good sign.

Incidentally, I still have my hiccoughs.

FROM *Benchley—or Else!*

The Literary Treatment of Insomnia

SAUL JARCHO

Newspaper articles and government reports constantly remind us that the citizens of the United States consume huge and steadily increasing amounts of somniferous drugs. The quantities, whether reckoned in grams or dollars, are appalling. The manifest dangers which threaten a chronically half-narcotized nation have encouraged the search for alternative methods of producing sleep, preferably drugless.

The first that comes to mind is the use of tape-recorded sermons or lectures. Since diatribes against sin often banish wakefulness on a Sunday morning, it is reasonable to think that the same effect might be obtained on a weekday night. Those who are averse to theology, both diurnal and nocturnal, would do well to consider instead such subjects as stratigraphy or embryology. A discourse on crustal deformation or on the troubles of the mesonephros is the equal of at least three grains of seconal—and produces no after-effects.

While the merits of the tape-recorded lecture are established beyond cavil this method has a few inconveniences. The equipment is expensive and sometimes troublesome. Even more important is the problem of recording. Can one be certain that one's favourite somniferous preacher or lecturer is at his dullest on the day when the tape-recorder is surreptitiously brought into action? For these reasons the use of tape-recordings has not got far and the search for other methods has continued.

Many years ago the *Harvard Crimson* introduced an annual unpopularity contest in order to ascertain, by genuinely democratic methods, what was the world's worst poem. Usually the palm was awarded to one of the works of Dante or Cervantes or Wordsworth. It stands to reason that in these writings must lie the object of our quest. The list can easily be amplified and improved.

The appropriateness of Dante for the treatment of insomnia cannot be doubted. I speak here only of the *Inferno*, since no one ever reaches the *Purgatorio* or the *Paradiso*. The narcotic properties of the *Inferno* depend on the theme and structure of the poem. The reader is first led gently downward and is then drawn round in circles—all this in gloom and darkness—until consciousness vanishes. The same introductory cantos have the same hypnotic effect night after night.

It is easy to prove that the *Inferno* is an effective remedy for sleeplessness. Look at any copy of the book and you will observe that all the wear and tear is in the first few pages; the later pages look fresh and new.

As for Wordsworth, he is an author whom I hesitate to recommend in a comparatively mild disease like insomnia. Wordsworth should be read only after one has fallen asleep, but it is difficult to see how this can be done. To this rule there is one exception, viz. that Wordsworth may be read in revised versions, such as that written by the late lamented Franklin P. Adams:

> She lived unknown, and few could know
>   When Lucy ceased to be;
> But she is in her grave. Ho! ho!
>   Tee hee! tee hee!

As for Cervantes, the perpetually delicate state of our relations with Latin countries precludes further comment. Nor would I dare to displease personages at Whitehall by reflections on Bright's Anglo-Saxon Grammar.

There remain for consideration the underestimated resources of medical literature. For the relief of insomnia treatises on anatomy are wonderful. Who can read Gallaudet on fascia (New York, 1931) without becoming involved in mesodermal labyrinths until consciousness takes flight? And even an insomniac anatomist who should grapple with W. S. Miller on the anatomy of the lung (Springfield, 1937) will find that he will his quietus take.

But both of these books not only ablate consciousness, they threaten respiration and even life itself;

hence they are recommended for the severest cases only. It remains to mention one volume which is guaranteed to produce prolonged peaceful and dreamless sleep, equivalent to the deeper planes of anaesthesia. This is the treatise by Schmorl and Junghanns, *Die Gesunde und Kranke Wirbelsaule im Rontgenbild* (Leipzig, 1932). Throughout its pages there is nothing to arouse so much as a flicker even from the most ardent devotee of osteopathology, and the reader can plod on from *Zwischenwirbelscheiben* to *Lendenkreuzbeingegend* without having his attention once aroused. But few if any will ever get that far.

FROM *Punch,* June 15, 1960

CHAPTER VI

Good Company for Your Misery

Millions live in daily fear of the dentist's drill and the doctor's bill. They live with the terrible anxiety of knowing that their symptoms are those of at least twelve terminal diseases. Or, perfectly healthy, they hourly face the gnawing expectation of some new onslaught of infirmity. Or, when their fears finally find some basis in fact (usually an ulcer), they exaggerate their illnesses with wild flights of fantasy that send them scurrying to make out their wills and to purchase cemetery plots.

There is really very little anyone can say to comfort one of them, but they do get some solace out of communing with others of their kind. And if that person should be as famous and successful as Goodman Ace—a self-proclaimed hypochondriac for fun and profit—well then, so much the better.

Another kindred spirit is Stern, the woeful antihero of Bruce Jay Friedman's novel, which bears his name as its title.

How many of you have dreamed of telling your doctor to mind his own business when he tells you to quit smoking and drinking, or to watch your diet? And how many of you ladies have fondly wished for something really witty to say to your gynecologists? You might want to take a few hints in the first category from the irreplaceable Sir Winston Churchill, and in the second from Cornelia Otis Skinner. The latter's "Address to the American Gynecological Society" is a classic of the hilarious double-entendre.

So whether it's illustrious company you seek, or vicarious pleasure, or just a good laugh, I know you'll find it in this next section.

Address to the
American Gynecological Society
CORNELIA OTIS SKINNER

Ladies and gentlemen of the profession . . . if not the oldest in the world, at least one of the most time-honored. You find me in a more awkward position than any in which I have ever been placed by certain of your distinguished members. I am as bewildered by my presence here as you must be. In fact I feel as uncertain of the issue as I did on an occasion when, giving a monologue performance a number of years ago in a New England town, I started off under the handicap of a far from encouraging introduction. (I rather liked this introduction because it is such a fine example of New England's traditional thrift.) The lady of the organization which was . . . having me . . . (that highly obstetrical expression!) rose and with fluttering apology said "Ladies and gentlemen, owing to the high price of Rear Admiral Byrd, we have Miss Skinner with us this evening." Well, let's face it . . . you have Miss Skinner with you this evening and it's not owing to the high price of any of the fees you have charged me over the years.

As I understand it, the yearly address to this learned gathering should be of an instructive or enlightening nature. It is an odd and I must admit a somewhat pleasurable sensation to be in the position of offering advice to the physician.

Well, whether or not you'll take mine, I think this a golden opportunity for giving the medical profession a bit of the patient's point of view. In other words to hear from the person at the other end of the . . . shall we say the stereopticon? As the humble presenter of this angle . . . this seldom heard from point of view (I am referring to opinion, not position) I really feel, without undue modesty, that I am a good choice. Over the years I have had the privilege . . . or shall we call it the dubious pleasure . . . of considerable contact with your branch of the profession, due to the fact that *my* profession has obliged me to travel extensively throughout the length and breadth of the United States, and that the birth of a son, plus certain defects of my anatomy, have required frequent consultations, inspections and repairs to the extent that, in the words of Somerset Maugham, you have left me only the bare necessities of life. I have perhaps had more experience than most patients . . . (I'd rather say "clients" . . . the word "patient" immediately reduces me to a state of apprehension and general debility) . . . I have had more opportunities to see you at work . . . if see is what I mean . . . to compare your methods, your relationships with your clients . . . your manners . . . your bedside ones, your desk-side ones and your table-side ones. And I have also had occasion to speculate as to how much you know . . . not of your science . . . but of the point of view of your clientele.

Of course, during your first years of internship you must all have grown callous to the shocks of your profession, but I must tell you (and I am hereby appointing myself spokesman for us beneficiaries of that profession) that we don't easily grow accustomed to such shocks. For the nicely brought-up girl, there is something that is hard to reconcile with her genteel sensibilities about walking into the inner sanctum of a complete stranger, solemnly describing her symptoms and at the end of the recital hearing the stranger say "Will you please go into the next room and take off everything except your shoes and stockings?" It wouldn't seem so bad if it weren't for that shoes and stockings clause! To my impressionable mind it has always smacked of the more erotic refinements of Berlin during its decadence. Be it to the honor of my upbringing, I have always kept on not only my shoes and stockings, but also my hat! If a costume made up of a sheet and a John Fredericks model is not the smartest of attire, God knows it's the most respectable. Even after the sheet has been put to the same sort of use as the old-fashioned photographer's black cloth, the hat remains as the badge of womanly modesty, triumphant over the most distressing of positions.

You know, I married a sportsman. During the first years of married life, I tried valiantly to become a horsewoman . . . a terrifying period which drove me in desperation into becoming a mother. In other words, having learned to put my feet forward into the stirrups, I soon learned the reverse. And from that vantage point . . . those vantage points . . . I had widespread opportunity to observe and compare your varying techniques. I speak, of course, less of medical or surgical techniques than social. It takes all sorts of people to

make a world and it takes all sorts of doctors to make
a profession . . . (I almost said . . . a patient). There
is the frighteningly eminent doctor . . . the sort who
is to medicine what Darryl Zanuck is to motion pictures. In other words who is so famous he never appears on the set until everything is made ready for
his entrance . . . which is often impressively delayed
until the actors begin to wonder if he ever will. And
just as you're about to become righteously indignant,
he appears, by which time you're in a position in which
you can't resist. This sort of doctor is apt to be also the
monosyllabic type . . . or even the silent type doctor.
During his period of exploration, he never makes a
single comment, never utters a word, never smiles,
never even goes tchk-tchk-tchk! After the examination
he rises abruptly and with noncommittal solemnity,
stalks out of the room leaving you with the nurse who
tells you that as soon as you've dressed, Dr. Famous
will see you in his private office. Of course, you immediately think that what he's found out is so appalling, it defies even the discoveries of Wassermann . . .
it's something too awful for even the nurse to hear.

I knew one woman who was finally able to thaw
down the cold front of this particularly uncommunica-
tive type. It was around Christmas time, she was very
great with child and she was determined to get some
sort of response from her deadpan medico whom we
might as well call Dr. Smith. So, with cunning ingenuity she wrote in lipstick across her teemingly fruit-
ful tummy "Merry Xmas, Dr. Smith." Be it to the face-
saving credit of the profession that Dr. Smith did laugh.

Then there is the opposite type. The chatty physician.

The sort who asks if you've read any good books lately or when did you last see the Joneses . . . all of which would be extremely pleasant if he didn't carry on such animated chit-chat all the time he's going with gun and camera into the Heart of Darkness. There's another fascinating thing about the chatty type. Quite often it happens that if you run across them socially at some cocktail party or what have you, they don't recognize you. It comes as quite a shock to discover the flaw in these genial gentlemen. Maybe theirs is a case of "I never remember a name, but . . ."

Then there is the singing or crooner type doctor . . . the sort who in the spirit of Disney's Snow White whistles while he works. This, I may say, is my favorite type. He shall be nameless but easily recognized and he's sitting right here in this room. He has a way of singing while he works . . . which, while most endearing to his clientele who knows and therefore loves him well, is apt to be a bit confusing to the uninitiated. My secretary, a wonderful Irish gal, had occasion to consult him about some one of those minor ills which a Victorian heritage still obliges us to refer to with lowered eyes as "a woman's trouble." She listened for a time to the doctor's cheery vocalizing then looked . . . down . . . happily at him and said "Glory be to God, Doctor, you sure love your work." Another uninitiate was the wife of the fine Negro band leader Count Basie. Mrs. Basie . . . (or should one say the Countess Basie?) hearing our charming Bing Crosby of the forceps doin' his stuff, suddenly interrupted him in the midst of his researches to enquire politely "Doctor, just give me that down-beat again."

Now, Gentlemen (I say gentlemen because while I am well aware of the number of feminine members of the brotherhood-sisterhood there are, the harvest of my experience has been gleaned chiefly from the brothers), there is one aspect of your business of which you know nothing whatsoever and regarding which I believe it's high time you were made aware . . . of. And that is what goes on in your waiting-rooms . . . particularly when they are replete with women who in turn, are replete with child. Of course none of you ever pause to see . . . when occasionally you make an impressive dash from your outer door to your inner office—because you're late or because you couldn't face the prospect of looking at us all, or because you've an emergency phone-call, or because you're just plain late. Women in the office of an obstetrician have a behavior all their own. It's a continuous scene of mutual inspection and speculation. One eventually gets accustomed every two weeks or so to seeing the same old familiar faces . . . but the old familiar contours are a constant source of interest far more fascinating than those old copies of Life, Time and the New Yorker which must have been read by all the members of a doctor's family, thumbed up, torn and jumped upon and eventually placed on the table of his waiting-rooms. The obstetrician's waiting-room is the one place of gathering where women inspect not each other's clothes . . . but each other's outlines. A new-comer enters, the eyes of the waiting sorority go straight to the midriff.

You know, you can do some pretty fancy calculating if you know how and what to observe. The beginner, as

one might call her, comes blithely in, her hat at a smart
angle, picks up one of those mangled periodicals,
chooses either the sofa or an armchair, and relaxes into
its depths. When her turn is called, she leaps nimbly to
her feet, drops the periodical, picks it up with easy agil-
ity and skips in through the inner door. The more advanced . . . both in regard to condition and shape
. . . say the 5 to 6 monthers, enter in slower motion.
That same chic hat has gone further back on the head.
She picks up a periodical (undoubtedly the same one
as before) chooses a more upright chair, sits with less
abandon and when her turn is called, rises slowly,
drops the periodical, stoops to pick it up, but finding
she can't reach it, bends her knees and retracts it, and
with injured dignity plods through the inner door. Last
scene of all that ends this strange, eventful history is
Mother Nature-Ceres who waddles in, her hat, this
time on the back of her head, as if to balance all that
precedes her . . . picks up that same copy of Life,
looks about for a place to sit down and finding no possible contour model, perches gingerly on the arm of
the armchair, when her turn comes, again drops the
magazine, again tries to pick it up forward, sideways,
at an angle, even knee-bending, utters a mental "To
hell with it!" and waddles majestically through that
inner door.

Another aspect of the waiting-room I'd like to mention is the receptionist nurse. She has a cozy way of
talking shop with the more loquacious clients . . .
and she does so in a jargon that seems peculiar to the
race of obstetrical nurses. "Mrs. Brown delivered last
night," she'll tell someone brightly, or "We're expecting

Mrs. White to deliver before tomorrow" . . . (that mail-carrier phraseology . . . "Neither rain nor heat," etc.). Then she uses another interesting term . . . she'll say "We've been having a run on girls lately" or "Better hurry, Mrs. Robinson, we're in the midst of a run on boys!" However, she is always a pleasant and sympathetic person . . . always most co-operative, especially when it comes to that sporadic little drama that is enacted at the beginning of these visits . . . when a patient comes in and, with arch discretion, the receptionist asks "Mrs. Jones, have you something for me?" Sometimes a crisis arises when Mrs. Jones, in sudden panic, realizes she hasn't . . . but someone else may have . . . in which event, there is a whispered consultation between Mrs. Jones and the receptionist which ends in the receptionist picking up the phone, dialing a number and an ensuing conversation which may go somewhat like this . . . "Hello? Schrafft's restaurant? I'm calling for Mrs. Cadwaller Jones. She was there for lunch today and she thinks she may have left a small parcel . . . second table to the left."

Of course, conditions may have changed. It was 23 years ago that I began these exhaustive researches . . . or rather that they were begun on me. When I was in what is laughingly known as the state of expectant motherhood, I was also in a state of having to fulfill the obligations of a theatrical tour. (The actress' greatest difficulty is the acquiring of proper timing. Dramatic critics manage these things better. John Mason Brown's second son, he tells me, was born between *Charley's Aunt* and *George Washington Slept Here*.) For five months, I and Little Nemo toured the

Middle-West trailing clouds of sweetness, light and nausea. Being neither a pioneer nor a Mme. Schumann-Heink, for whom it was apparently nothing to be a Rhine maiden one evening and the next morning the mother of a new little Heink, I don't recommend a lyceum tour as the best of regimens.

All nonsense aside, I can't tell you how happy and proud I am that you should have chosen me to speak to you this evening. Surely yours must be the most rewarding of all the branches of medicine . . . the happiness you bring us, the health and new life you restore to us. As self-appointed spokesman . . . spokeswoman . . . for my sisterhood, may I tell you of our gratitude and affection . . . I'll even say our love . . . (you know it is true that every new mother falls in love for a time with her obstetrician). May I herewith propose a toast from the ladies of America in words which are singularly apt . . . gentlemen of the profession, BOTTOMS UP!!!

FROM *Bottoms Up!*

Dental or Mental, I Say It's Spinach
S. J. PERELMAN

A few days ago, under the heading, Man Leaps Out Window As Dentist Gets Forceps, *The New York Times* reported the unusual case of a man who leaped out a window as the dentist got the forceps. Briefly, the circumstances were these. A citizen in Staten Island tottered into a dental parlor and, indicating an aching molar, moaned, "It's killing me. You've got to pull it out." The dentist grinned like a Cheshire cat—*The New York Times* neglected to say so, but a Cheshire cat who was present at the time grinned like a dentist— and reached for his instruments. "There was a leap and a crash," continues the account. "The astonished dentist saw his patient spring through the closed window and drop ten feet to the sidewalk, where he lay dazed." The casualty was subsequently treated at a near-by hospital for abrasion and shock by Drs. J. G. Abrazian and Walter Shock, and then, like a worm, crept back to the dentist, apologized and offered to pay for the damage. On one point, however, he remained curiously adamant. He still has his tooth.

As a party who recently spent a whole morning with his knees braced against a dentist's chest, whimpering "Don't—don't—I'll do anything, but don't drill!" I am probably the only man in America equipped to sympathize with the poor devil. Ever since Nature presented me at birth with a set of thirty-two flawless little pearls of assorted sizes, I never once relaxed my vigilant stewardship of same. From the age of six onward, I constantly polished the enamel with peanut brittle, massaged the incisors twice daily with lollipops, and chewed taffy and chocolate-covered caramels faithfully to exercise the gums. As for consulting a dentist regularly, my punctuality practically amounted to a fetish. Every twelve years I would drop whatever I was doing and allow wild Caucasian ponies to drag me to a reputable orthodontist. I guess you might say I was hipped on the subject of dental care.

When, therefore, I inadvertently stubbed a tooth on a submerged cherry in an old-fashioned last week and my toupee ricocheted off the ceiling, I felt both dismayed and betrayed. By eleven the next morning, I was seated in the antechamber of one Russell Pipgrass, D.D.S., limply holding a copy of the *National Geographic* upside down and pretending to be absorbed in Magyar folkways. Through the door communicating with the arena throbbed a thin, blood-curdling whine like a circular saw biting into a green plank. Suddenly an ear-splitting shriek rose above it, receding into a choked gurgle. I nonchalantly tapped out my cigarette in my eardrum and leaned over to the nurse, a Medusa type with serpents writhing out from under her prim white coif.

"Ah—er—pardon me," I observed, swallowing a bit of emery paper I had been chewing. "Did you hear anything just then?"

"Why, no," she replied, primly tucking back a snake under her cap. "What do you mean?"

"A kind of scratchy sound," I faltered.

"Oh, that," she sniffed carelessly. "Impacted wisdom tooth. We have to go in through the skull for those, you know." Murmuring some inconsequential excuse about lunching with a man in Sandusky, Ohio, I dropped to the floor and was creeping toward the corridor on all fours when Doctor Pipgrass emerged, rubbing his hands. "Well, here's an unexpected windfall!" he cackled, his eyes gleaming with cupidity. "Look out— slam the door on him!" Before I could dodge past, he pinioned me in a hammer lock and bore me, kicking and struggling, into his web. He was trying to wrestle me into the chair when the nurse raced in, brandishing a heavy glass ash tray.

"Here, hit him with this!" she panted.

"No, no, we mustn't bruise him," muttered Pipgrass. "Their relatives always ask a lot of silly questions." They finally made me comfy by strapping me into the chair with a half dozen towels, tilted my feet up and pried open my teeth with a spoon. "Now then, where are his X-rays?" demanded the doctor.

"We haven't any," returned the nurse. "This is the first time he's been here."

"Well, bring me any X-rays," her employer barked. "What difference does it make? When you've seen one tooth, you've seen them all." He held up the X-rays against the light and examined them critically. "Well, friend, you're in a peck of trouble," he said at length. "You might as well know the worst. These are the teeth of an eighty-year-old man. You got here just in time." Plucking a horrendous nozzle from the rack, he shot compressed air down my gullet that sent me into a strangled paroxysm, and peered curiously at my inlays.

"Who put those in, a steamfitter?" he sneered. "You ought to be arrested for walking around with a job like that." He turned abruptly at the rustle of greenbacks and glared at his nurse. "See here, Miss Smedley, how many times have I told you not to count the patient's money in front of him? Take the wallet outside and go through it there." She nodded shamefacedly and slunk out. "That's the kind of thing that creates a bad impression on the layman," growled Doctor Pipgrass, poking at my tongue with a sharp stick. "Now what seems to be the trouble in there?"

"Ong ong ong," I wheezed.

"H'm'm'm, a cleft palate," he mused. "Just as I feared. And you've got between four and five thousand cavities. While we're at it, I think we'd better tear out those lowers with a jackhammer and put in some nice expensive crowns. Excuse me." He quickly dialed a telephone number. "Is that you, Irene?" he asked. "Russell. Listen, on that white mink coat we were talking about at breakfast—go right ahead, I've changed my mind . . . No, I'll tell you later. He's filthy with it."

"Look, doctor," I said with a casual yawn. "It's nothing really—just a funny tickling sensation in that rear tooth. I'll be back Tuesday—a year from Tuesday."

"Yes, yes," he interrupted, patting me reassuringly. "Don't be afraid now; this won't hurt a bit." With a slow, cunning smile, he produced from behind his back a hypodermic of the type used on brewery horses and, distending my lip, plunged it into the gum. The tip of my nose instantly froze, and my tongue took on the proportions of a bolt of flannel. I tried to cry out, but my larynx was out to lunch. Seizing the opportunity, Pipgrass snatched up his drill, took a firm purchase on my hair and teed off. A mixture of sensation roughly comparable to being alternately stilettoed and inflated with a bicycle pump overcame me; two thin wisps of smoke curled upward slowly from my ears. Fortunately, I had been schooled from boyhood to withstand pain without flinching, and beyond an occasional scream that rattled the windows, I bore myself with the stoicism of a red man. Scarcely ninety minutes later, Doctor Pipgrass thrust aside the drill, wiped his streaming forehead and shook the mass of protoplasm before him.

"Well, we're in the home stretch," he announced brightly, extracting a rubber sheet from a drawer. "We'll put this dam on you and fill her in a jiffy. You don't get claustrophobia, do you?"

"Wh-what's that?" I squeaked.

"Fear of being buried alive," he explained smoothly. "Kind of a stifling feeling. Your heart starts racing and you think you're going crazy. Pure imagination, of course." He pinned the rubber sheet over my face, slipped it over the tooth and left me alone with my thoughts. In less time than it takes to relate, I was a graduate member, *summa cum laude*, of the green, my heart was going like Big Ben, and a set of castanets in my knees was playing the "Malagueña." Summoning my last reserves of strength, I cast off my bonds and catapulted through the anteroom to freedom. I bequeathed Pipgrass a fleece-lined overcoat worth sixty-eight dollars, and he's welcome to it; I'll string along nicely with this big wad of chewing gum over my tooth. On me it looks good.

FROM Perelman's Home Companion

Churchill and the Battles of Medicine

LORD MORAN

August 6, 1944

Now that we are going to Italy in August, there is the question of malaria. I had a presentiment that the battle for mepacrine[1] would have to be fought all over again.

I determined to get my facts right—it avoids a massacre. I went for them to Millbank.[2]

"Whatever else he does in Italy," they said, "he must take mepacrine as a safeguard against malaria."

As I made my way along the Embankment I could find no flaw in their arguments. I wanted to avoid, if I could, a pitched battle with the P.M. After all, he has enough trouble, without my adding to it. He will always listen to advice if the reasoning seems to him sound—it is futile, of course, to lay down the law—though I am careful to administer it in small doses and —this is important—I only give him the draught when we are alone.

So next morning I went to the Annexe soon after nine o'clock, knowing by experience that I was likely to find him alone at that hour. When I had said my piece, he glowered at me. Mepacrine, he was told,

1. Mepacrine or hydrochloride atebrin is a synthetic anti-malarial drug, which was widely used for prophylaxis and treatment during the Second World War, when there was a shortage of quinine.

2. Army Medical College, Millbank, London.

made people quite ill. And, anyway, he thought it was quite unnecessary. I stuck to my point, leaving him to think it over. When I had gone he telephoned Buckingham Palace, and the answer came back. "The King knows nothing about mepacrine." He hadn't taken anything at all when in Italy. Winston is just incorrigible. He has only to press a bell to bring into the room the greatest malarial experts in the world; instead, he turns his back on science and asks the King whether he ought to take mepacrine when he visits Italy. When the P.M.'s doubts were confirmed in this fashion he sent a telegram to Alex in Italy to elicit his views. I first heard of this when the P.M. sent me Alex's reply:

"Top Secret.
"Special Unnumbered Signal.
"7.0.0. 1025. 4th August.
"Top Secret and personal for Prime Minister from General Alexander.

"My doctors tell me that these yellow pills do not prevent malaria but only suppress it temporarily. They upset some people considerably. Whilst I cannot guarantee you immunity from malaria, I think you may regard the risk as slight. Neither I nor my staff take pills and we have virtually no malaria at my headquarters. I suggest you tell the doctors to keep their pills. If you have Mess wellingtons or mosquito boots, bring them with you for evening wear."

When I had collected ammunition I fired my gun at the Prime Minister. I began with figures. I explained that during the first two months of the Sicilian campaign last year we lost the effective strength of two infantry divisions from malaria. In the campaign in New

Guinea half the force were evacuated sick in six months —47,534 of 95,050 men, whereas there were only 3,140 battle casualties. Those in command agreed that this wastage from malaria could have been avoided, for if mepacrine were taken regularly there was little or no malaria. It was simply a question of discipline, of a drill for the administration of mepacrine. The principle was laid down that commanders would be held personally responsible for malarial wastage. As for Alex, when he proclaimed to the Prime Minister that neither he nor any of his staff set an example to their men by taking the pills themselves, he may not have known that it was a court-martial offence in the Army in Italy under his command to omit mepacrine drill.

The instruction of Winston is not without its own hazards, and I thought it prudent to close on a lighter note. The postscript to my letter read: "General Alexander suggests the doctors keep their pills. I venture to wonder if General Alexander's views on medical matters have the same value as mine on military affairs."

The P.M. lost no time in replying to this blast:

"Most Immediate.
"Secret.
"Telephone Message 6th August 1944 from the Prime Minister to Lord Moran.
"In view of your salvo, all surrender unconditionally and hoist the yellow flag."

After that sally, how could anyone be out of temper?

September 21, 1944

Winston made some gurgling sounds in his throat. "Do you know the yarn of the man who was castrated?"

More gurgling. "A man called Thomson went to a surgeon and asked him to castrate him. The surgeon demurred, but when the man persisted and argued he eventually agreed, and took him into hospital. The morning after the operation Thomson woke up in great discomfort. He noticed that the man in the next bed was in pain and was groaning. He leant towards him over the side of the bed. 'What did they do to you,' he called. The man replied: 'I've been circumcised.' 'Good Lord,' Thomson exclaimed, 'that's the word I couldn't remember when the surgeon asked me what I wanted done.'"

The P.M.'s face screwed up into creases and he made some crowing, expiratory sounds in his throat as he did when really amused.

"I shall use that story," he said, "when they give me my degree. I'll bring it in by urging the importance of precision of language. Oh, they'll never report it. They couldn't."

June 27, 1946

"A short time ago I was ready to retire and die gracefully. Now I'm going to stay and have them out." With great vehemence: "I'll tear their bleeding entrails out of them. I'm in pretty good fettle," he went on in a more subdued tone. "The Jerome blood." [1]

"You would," I mocked, "ascribe to natural causes what is due to my art."

"Ah, no, Charles," he said warmly. "I saw Alexander Fleming about my eyes. He wasn't interested in me as

1. Leonard Jerome, Churchill's American maternal grandfather: died, 1891.

a patient, but in a very unusual bug in my nose, a staphylococcus, which was very resistant to penicillin." With a grin. "The bug seems to have caught my truculence. This is its finest hour."

FROM *Churchill: Taken from the Diaries of Lord Moran*

The Fine Art of Hypochondria
GOODMAN ACE

I didn't become a hypochondriac until late in my middle twenty-five years—if you will fantasize along with me that a man's life span is seventy-five and is divided into three equal spans of twenty-five. So by the time I was forty I was an apprentice hypochondriac and by the time I reached forty-two, full-blown. At the age of fifty-two I stopped fighting it, accepted senescence as a way of life. And now, some years later, I am making this report to my fellow sufferers.

My symptoms were simple, really. At any given moment and all through any day or night I could develop a rapid heartbeat and pulse that triggered a shortness of breath accompanied by a fear of dying. It was not so much the actual fear of dying as it was doing it unattractively; lying prone on a strange, busy street somewhere or slumped in a theater seat, or in a restaurant or a crowded elevator, in a cab or in the home of friends, on a beach or in the snow, in a radio studio or in a doctor's office.

It is with the purpose of demonstrating that there

is an art to handling hypochondria with grace and
dignity that this piece is being written. Fainting in
nightclubs, regurgitating in taxis, leaning against tall
buildings are not accepted *savoir-faire*. I know. I was
there, Charlie. I was a mess.

Medical schools weren't turning out doctors fast
enough for me. Most of the doctors to whom I came
crawling for help curtly told me after thorough examinations that there was nothing wrong with me. I made
short shrift of them. But I do remember three of my
early doctors fondly and with reverence. Of all the
medicos to whose offices I beat paths in those years,
they were the most patient, they were kindly, and
they were always in attendance when I needed them.
They at least satisfied my need for knowing that something was really wrong with me by separately diagnos-
ing my case as neurocirculatory aesthenia.

Whatever all that meant, at least I had something to
go on. It's no picnic having something physically wrong
with you and not having a name for it. So I struggled
on with my neurocirculatory aesthenia as best I could.
If somebody remarked "Haven't seen you in a long
time," I knew he meant "What hospital have you been
in?" I began to find reasons for not going out. I began
lying down a lot. As an excuse, I was once in bed for
nine days with a bad haircut. What I needed was some
new doctors. I found them.

One day I was in the office of one of the new doctors
who had x-rayed me and turned my stomach inside
out. For fear he might dismiss me as having nothing
wrong with me, I confided that what I had was neurocirculatory aesthenia. To my delight he nodded his

head. The symptoms, he told me, were a rapid heart-beat and pulse.

Needless to say, I was shaken. I asked if he could give me something for that. He wrote a prescription. I stuck it in my pocket and walked out. At the first drug-store, I approached the pharmacist, took the prescription out, and was about to hand it to him when I read what he had written: "You have no organic abnormality of the heart, no feeling of breathlessness is dangerous, nothing bad will happen to you." And he had the nerve to sign it. I ordered a tube of toothpaste—small size. I knew now I wasn't going to last long.

FROM *The Fine Art of Hypochondria*

The Ulcer

BRUCE JAY FRIEDMAN

Stern's doctor sent him first to a man with a forest of golden curls named Brewer who took pictures of his belly. Brewer had said, "Come very early; it's the only way I can get a lot of people in," and when Stern arrived, he filled him first with thick, maltlike substances, then put him inside an eyelike machine, and, taking his place on the other side of it, said, "Think of delicious dishes. Your favorites."

Stern was barefooted and wore a thin shift; the light in the streets had not yet come up and his eyes were crusted with sleep. "I may be sick," he said. "How can I think of delicious things? All right, eggs."

"Don't fool around," said the man, squinting into the machine. "I've got to get a lot of people in. Give me your favorite taste temptations; otherwise the pictures will be grainy."

"I really do like eggs," Stern said. "Late at night, when I've been out, I'd rather have them than anything."

"Are you trying to make a monkey out of me?" the man screamed, darting away from the machine. "Do you know how many I have got to get in today? *You give me your favorites*." He flew at Stern, fat fists clenched, blond curls shaking, like a giant, enraged baby, and Stern, frightened, said, "Soufflés, soufflés."

"That ought to do it," said the man, his eye to the machine again. "I'm not sending out any grainy pictures."

A week after the stomach pictures had been taken, Stern sat alongside an old woman with giant ankles in the outer office of Fabiola, the specialist, and it occurred to him that he would hear all the really bad news in his life in this very office; there would be today's and then, at some later date, news of lung congestions and then, finally, right here in this very room with the wallpaper and leather couches that seemed specially designed for telling people hopeless things, he would get the final word, the news that would wrap up the ball game forever. The woman beside him sorrowfully tapped her feet to an obscure Muzak ballad and, although Stern knew it was cruel, he could not help passing along his observation.

"This is a room for bad things," he said. "All the

bad news in your life you get right here, right to the very end."

"I can't think now," she said, tapping away. "Not with these feet I can't."

Stern felt ashamed when he was called ahead of the giant-ankled woman, but then it occurred to him that perhaps her ankles had always been that way and were not swollen and enfeebled but sturdy with rocklike peasant power. Perhaps within her there raged fifty years more of good health; Stern was being called first because he was much further downhill, the slimness of his ankles notwithstanding.

Fabiola was a tall, brisk man who wore loose-flowing clothes and lived in the shadow of an old doctor whose practice he had taken over, the famed Robert Lualdi, a handsome, Gable-like man who had been personal physician to Ziegfeld beauties. Somewhat senile and in retirement now, the elderly Luadli, nevertheless, would drop in at odd times during the day, often while examinations were in session, put his feet on the young doctor's desk, and reminisce about the days when he had a practice that was "really hotcha." Once, when Fabiola was examining a young woman's chest, the old man had come into the room, pronounced her breasts "honeys," and then gone winking out the door. The interruptions kept the young doctor on edge, and he had developed a brisk style, as though trying always to wind things up and thereby head off one of the elder doctor's nostalgic visits. He was holding the pictures of Stern's stomach up to the light when Stern entered, fingers dug into his great belly, as though to prevent the parachute within from blossoming out further. "You've got one in there, all right," said Fabiola. "Beauty. You ought to see the crater. That's the price we pay for civilization."

"Got what?" Stern asked.

"An ulcer."

"Oh," said Stern. He was sorry he had let the doctor talk first; it was as though if he had burst in immediately and told Fabiola what kind of a person he was, how nice and gentle, he might have been able to convince him that he was mistaken, that Stern was simply not the kind of fellow to have an ulcer. It was as though the doctor had a valise full of them, was dealing them out to certain kinds of people, and would revoke them if presented with sound reasons for doing so. Political influence might persuade the doctor to take it back, too. Once, when Stern had been unable to get into college, his uncle had reached a Marine colonel named Treadwell, who had phoned the college and smoothed his admission. Stern felt now that if only Treadwell were to call the doctor, Fabiola would call back the ulcer and give it to someone more deserving.

"Look, I don't think I want to have one of them," Stern said, getting a little dizzy, still feeling that it was all a matter of debate and that he wasn't going to get his point across. "I'm thirty-four." When the doctor heard his age, he would immediately see that he had the wrong man and apologize for inconveniencing Stern.

"That's when they start showing up. Look, we don't have to go in there if that's what you're worried about. We get at them other ways."

"What do you mean, go in there?" said Stern. Going in there was different from simply operating. He had a vision of entire armadas of men and equipment trooping into his stomach and staying there a long time. "You mean there was even a chance you might have had to go in?"

"I don't see any reason to move in," said Fabiola. The old doctor opened the door then and, with eyes narrowed, said, "I knew I heard some tootsies in here." He limped in rakishly and took a seat next to Stern. "Excuse me," he said, "I thought you were a tootsie. My office was always full of 'em. The real cheese, too."

"I think I may be pretty sick," Stern said, and the old man rose and said, "Oh, excuse. I'll be getting along. Well, boys, keep everything hotcha. Any tootsies, you know who to call."

"Hotcha, hotcha," he said, and winked his way out the door.

"Look," Stern said, leaning forward now. "I really don't want to have one." He felt suddenly that it was all a giant mistake, that somehow the doctor had gotten the impression he didn't *mind* having one, that it made no difference to Stern one way or the other. This was his last chance to explain that he really didn't want to have one.

"I don't see what's troubling you," said Fabiola. "You'd think I'd said heart or something."

"Maybe it's the name," Stern said. "I can't even get myself to say it." It sounded to Stern like a mean little animal with a hairy face. *See the coarse-tufted, angry little ulcer, children. You must learn to avoid him because of his vicious temper. He is not nice like our friend the squirrel.* And here Stern had one running inside him. . . .

"I can see all of this if I'd said heart," Fabiola said, beginning to write. "All right, we'll get right at her. We can do it without moving in."

"Don't write," said Stern, searching for some last-ditch argument that would force Fabiola to reconsider. The writing would make it final. If he could get Fabiola to hold off on that, perhaps a last-minute call from Colonel Treadwell would clear him.

"I wear these tight pants," Stern said. "Really tight. I think the homosexuals are influencing all the clothes we wear, and it's silly, but I wear them anyway. I can hardly breathe, I wear them so tight. Do you think that might have done it?"

"No," said Fabiola, filling up little pieces of paper with furious scribbles. "You've definitely got one in there."

Once, on a scholarship exam, Stern had gotten stuck on the very first question. There were more than four hundred to go, but, instead of hurrying on to the next, he had continued for some reason to wrestle with the first, aware that time was flying. Unable to break through on the answer, he had felt a thickness start up in his throat and then had pitched forward on the floor, later to be revived in the girls' bathroom, all chances of passing the exam up in smoke. The same thickness formed in his throat now and he toppled forward into Fabiola's carpeting, not quite losing consciousness.

"I didn't say heart," Fabiola said, leaning forward. "I could understand if I'd said heart."

Helped to his feet, Stern felt better immediately. It was as though he had finally demonstrated how seriously he was opposed to having an ulcer.

"I think we ought to bed this one down for a while," the doctor said, writing again. "I know an inexpensive place. Can you get free?"

"Oh, Jesus, I've really got one then," said Stern, beginning to cry. "Can't you see that I don't want one? I'm thirty-four." Fabiola stood up and Stern looked at the doctor's softly rising paunch, encased in loose-flowing trousers, and wondered how he was able to keep it free of coarse-tufted, sharp-toothed little ulcers. Fabiola's belly had a stately, relaxed strength about it, and Stern wanted to hug it and tell the doctor about the kike man, how bad it was to drive past his house every night. Then perhaps the doctor would call the man, tell him the awful thing he'd done and that he'd better not do it any more. Or else Fabiola would ride out in a car and somehow, with the stately, dignified strength of his belly, bring the man to his knees.

"It's a nice little place upstate," said Fabiola, leading Stern to the door. "The way you hit the floor I think we ought to bed it down awhile. They'll be ready for you in about three days."

Stern wanted to protest. He wanted to say, "Wait a minute. You don't understand. I *really* don't want to have one. I'm not leaving this room until I don't have one any more." But the situation had become dreamlike, as though a man was coming for his throat with a razor and he was unable to cry out. "I just didn't want this," he heard himself say sweetly.

In the corridor, the old doctor winked at Stern and said, "You boys have a couple of tootsies in there?"

"I'm awfully sick," Stern said, and went out the door.

Crying in the street, Stern hailed a cab and gave the Negro driver, a scholarly-looking gentleman, his office address. "I've just been told I've got something lousy inside me," Stern said, still crying. "Jesus, how I don't want to have it in there."

"Cut him out," the man said, shaking his head emphatically, as though he were crying "Amen" at a good sermon. "He an ulcer, cut him out an' throw him 'pon the floor. He very strong, but you throw Mr. Ulcer 'pon the floor, you see how he like that. I got an uncle, he cut one, he live to be fifty-four."

Stern wanted to tell the man that fifty-four was no target to shoot for and that there'd be no cutting, either. He wanted to say that he thought the man's advice was terrible, but he was afraid the Negro, outwardly scholarly, had once fought as a welterweight and, irked, might quickly remove his horn-rims, back Stern against a fender, and cut him to ribbons with lethal combinations. When the cab pulled up, Stern said, "I might try cutting it out," and tipped the scholarly Negro handsomely.

FROM *Stern*

CHAPTER VII

Medical Mirth

Jokes and anecdotes about doctors are no different from jokes about anything else; they are mostly pretty poor. But there are a few good ones, and no anthology on medical humor would be truly complete without them. The laws of chance alone dictate that in the sampling that follows there will be at least several genuine rib-ticklers, but I hope that I have succeeded in bettering those odds.

A British professor wrote one day on his laboratory blackboard, "Professor Wilson informs his students that he has this day been appointed honorary physician to His Majesty, King Edward."

During the course of the class he was called from the room for a few moments, and on his return found that some wag had appended to his announcement these words: "God save the King."

A noted physician once visited a local asylum for the mentally ill, and, while passing through a corridor, he was approached by one of the inmates: "Take off your hat, sir!" cried the patient imperiously.

"Why should I?" asked the doctor.

"Because," replied the inmate, "I am a son of the Emperor of France."

"Oh. I beg your Royal Highness' pardon," said the physician placatingly, taking off his hat.

On returning to the asylum some time later, he was again accosted in the same corridor by the same patient, who again demanded, "Take off your hat, sir!"

"Why?" asked the doctor.

"Because I am the son of the Emperor of Germany" was the reply.

"Surely," asked the physician, "when I last had the honor of seeing your Royal Highness, you were the son of the Emperor of France?"

"Ah, yes," responded the inmate cannily, "but that was by another mother."

The doctor's phone rang at 2:30 A.M., and on the line was a man in a considerably agitated condition. "My wife, Doc!" he shouted. "I think it's her appendix. You'd better come over here in a hurry."

The doctor merely sighed patiently and told the man to calm himself and go back to bed. "Give her some bicarbonate of soda," he advised, "and I'll stop by tomorrow. Don't worry, it's not appendicitis."

But the husband protested that it was, in fact, appendicitis. The physician, now at the end of his patience, explained loudly, "Look, she can't have it. I took her appendix out three years ago. Did you ever hear of anyone having two appendixes?"

"Did you ever hear," replied the man, "of anybody having two wives?"

"You've got to help me, Doctor," said the patient frantically to his psychiatrist. "I can't remember anything for more than a few minutes. It's driving me crazy!"

"How long has this been going on?" the analyst inquired soothingly.

"How long has what been going on?" responded the patient.

Dr. Alfred Adler, the noted psychiatrist, was once giving a lecture on the theory that handicapped in-

dividuals frequently tend to specialize in their handicapped functions. Thus, explained the doctor, short-
winded boys tend to train themselves to become long-
distance runners, people with weak eyes tend to
become painters, and so forth. Adler concluded his
address and then threw the floor open to questions.

Immediately someone in the rear of the hall shouted,
"Dr. Adler, wouldn't your theory mean that weak-
minded people tend to become psychiatrists?"

Oliver St. John Gogarty, Ireland's great physician
and poet, was also a great punster. For example, when
he walked into a tavern and saw a friend wearing a
patch over one eye, he couldn't resist exclaiming, "Drink
to me with thine only eye!"

Gogarty's wit was probably sharpened considerably
by J. P. Mahaffy, one of his teachers at Trinity College.
It was Mahaffy who deftly bested his opponent, a lady,
when she finally concluded a lengthy argument favor-
ing woman's right to vote. "After all," she declared,
"what's the difference between a man and a woman?"

Mahaffy thought for a moment, then quietly replied,
"I can't conceive."

—*Medical World News*
May 14, 1965

The Reverend Francis Willis, an eighteenth-century
clergyman, was reputed to be very successful in his
treatment of cases of mental derangement. So great was
his stature that in 1788 he was called upon to adminis-

ter to King George III, who had undergone a complete mental collapse. Once, during the course of the treatment, the King asked Willis if, as a member of the clergy, he did not feel ashamed for practicing as a physician. Replied Willis, "Our Saviour, sir, went about healing the sick."

"Ah, yes," responded the King with a wry look, "but he didn't get 700 pounds for it—hey?"

An obviously nervous and excited young man came into the psychoanalyst's office constantly snapping his fingers and looking around him anxiously.

"Calm yourself," soothed the doctor. "Why are you doing that?"

"Because it keeps away the elephants," came the logical reply.

"But there aren't any elephants around here," protested the analyst.

"You see?" responded the young man. "It works."

Whenever a new discovery is reported to the scientific world, they say first, "It is probably not true." Thereafter, when the truth of the new proposition has been demonstrated beyond question, they say, "Yes, it may be true, but it is not important." Finally, when sufficient time has elapsed to fully evidence its importance, they say, "Yes, surely it is important, but it is no longer new."

—Michel de Montaigne

One of the many stories about the Doctors Mayo concerns the self-inflated Texas millionaire who, upon catching sight of Dr. Will, approached him with an air of great importance and asked, "Are you the head doctor here?"

"No," answered Dr. Will with exaggerated serious-ness. "My brother is the head doctor. I'm the belly doctor."

After an operation at a medical school, one student approached the eminent surgeon and asked him, "What did you operate on that man for?"

Replied the surgeon coolly, "$500."

Dear Abby: I am married and have seven children under 12 years of age. Recently I began working in a hospital, and my job brings me into close contact with X-ray equipment. Is it true that this will sterilize me?

DORIS

Dear Doris: I wouldn't bet on it.

Amused staff members of the Dorset County Hos-pital in Dorchester, England, reported the following account of a tonsillectomy as written by a seven-year-old tonsillectomee:

"When I went into the big room there were two lady angels all dressed in white. Then the two men angels came in the room.

"One of the men angels," continued the youngster, "looked down my throat and said, 'Lord! Look at that child's tonsils.'

"And the Lord looked, and said, 'I'll take them out at once.'"

One patient had tried every remedy and treatment that his doctor had prescribed, but had obtained no relief. Finally the doctor told him that he would have to go to see a specialist.

"But won't that be expensive?" asked the man apprehensively.

"Yes, I'm afraid it will," replied the doctor. "But it must be done."

"What will it cost?" asked the patient.

"Well, you will have to pay $25 for the first visit, and $5 for each visit after that."

The patient thought over his doctor's words for some time, and then called the recommended specialist. "Is this Dr. Stein, the specialist?" he asked.

"Yes, speaking," answered the physician.

"Well," began the patient, "here I am again."

There is one thing about baldness: it's neat.
                                        —Don Herald

A man and his wife entered the dentist's office. "I want to have a tooth pulled," announced the woman.

"And you don't have to bother with novocain or gas. We're in a bit of a rush."

"Well," said the surprised dentist, "you certainly are brave. Which tooth is it?"

"Henry," said the wife, turning to her husband, "show him your tooth."

A surgeon in a medical clinic was interviewing a new patient. "If I determine that an operation is necessary," asked the doctor, "would you have the money to pay for it?"

"Listen, Doctor," retorted the man, "if I didn't have the money to pay for it, would you find the operation necessary?"

Dr. Kenneth D. Keele, a London physician, once gave a lecture at Yale University in which he hypothesized that Mona Lisa's enigmatic smile was a result of her pregnant state. Dr. Allen S. Johnson, however, offered this alternative explanation in a letter to the *New England Journal of Medicine:*

"To one unencumbered by the sophistication of the obstetricians and historians, that smug, sly smile can only have one explanation: Mona Lisa has just discovered that she is *not* pregnant."

Having just given birth, a young woman was found poring over the telephone directory. The nurse asked her why, and the young woman replied that she was looking for a name for her baby. "But," suggested the nurse, "we have a wonderful little book which gives first names for both boys and girls."

"That's not what I'm looking for," answered the young mother. "I need a last name."

Some people are so sensitive that they feel snubbed if an epidemic overlooks them.

—Frank McKinney Hubbard

A psychologist was giving a young man some personality tests. Drawing a vertical line, he asked, "What does this make you think of?"

"Sex," answered the young man. Next the psychologist drew a circle. "And what does this make you think of?"

"Sex," was the response.

The psychologist drew a star. "And this?"

"Why, sex, of course," replied the young man.

"In my opinion," said the psychologist, putting down his pencil, "you have an obsession with sex."

"*I* have an obsession!" exclaimed the young man. "For goodness' sake, who's been drawing all those smutty pictures?"

A father and his bright four-year-old boy were out walking when they saw a huge, ugly man with a grotesquely bloated stomach. When the young lad asked his father why the man had such a big stomach, the father saw an opportunity to break his son of an unsavory habit. He told the boy that the man was deformed because he bit his nails, and that he too might become so deformed if he did not break his habit.

Some days later, the youngster's mother was giving a card party and invited her son in to meet all her guests. The boy began to greet each of the ladies, but soon he spied a woman who was plainly going to give birth in the near future.

"It's easy to see what *you've* been doing," cried the boy gleefully. Fortunately, the lad saved the entire party from eternal embarrassment by adding quickly, "You have been biting your nails."

Men are not going to embrace eugenics. They are going to embrace the first likely, trim-figured girl with limpid eyes and flashing teeth who comes along, in spite of the fact that her germ plasm is probably reeking with hypertension, cancer, haemophilia, color-blindness, hay fever, epilepsy, and amytrophic lateral sclerosis.

—Logan Clendening, M.D.

A worn and weary advertising executive was astonished when his doctor advised him to run the eight blocks from his apartment to his office each day, rolling a child's hoop. The physician explained that it was excellent therapy, and warned that if he didn't do it, he might be in danger of going to pieces entirely.

Alarmed at this possibility, the ad man bought a hoop and each day began rolling it to and from work, leaving it during the day in a nearby garage. At the end of one week he felt so much improved that he actually began to look forward to his "therapy." But one night, when he went to the garage to pick up his hoop, it was gone.

"I don't know how it could have happened, sir," apologized the garage manager, "but it's our responsibility, and we'll pay for it."

The executive was livid. "Pay for it!" he exploded. "Of course you'll pay for it. But what good is that going to do me? How in hell am I going to get home tonight?"

This verbal sally is reported to have taken place between the famous surgeon John Abernethy and one of his students during an oral examination.

Questioned Abernethy, "What would you do if a man was brought to you with a broken leg?"

"Set it, sir," was the reply.

"Good, very good. You're a very pleasant, witty young man; and doubtless you can tell me what muscles of the body I should set in motion if I kicked you as you deserve to be kicked for your impertinence?"

Answered the student, "You would set in motion the flexors and the extensors of my right arm, for I should immediately knock you down."

This sign was seen in a dentist's office: "Never select a set of dental plates from a window display. It is impolite to pick your teeth in public."

Alexandre Dumas once dined at the home of the celebrated Dr. Gistal in Marseilles. After the dinner, the physician brought in an autograph album for his distinguished guest to sign.

"Certainly," said Dumas, writing, "Since the famous Dr. Gistal began to practice here they have demolished the hospital . . ."

"Flattery!" exclaimed the doctor, quite pleased.

". . . and on its site made a cemetery," added Dumas.

Whenever I feel like exercise, I lie down until the feeling passes.

—Robert M. Hutchin

A highly agitated hypochondriac informed his doctor that he was suffering from a fatal disease of the liver.

"Nonsense!" retorted the physician. "You wouldn't know whether you had that or not. With that disease, there's no discomfort of any kind."

"I know," exclaimed the patient. "My symptoms exactly."

"Don't let the doctor frighten you," said the nurse, attempting to comfort a patient. "Doctors are like politicians—they view with alarm so that they can point with pride."

Samuel Hahnemann, founder of the homeopathic school of medicine, was once consulted by a wealthy

Englishman who explained his symptoms at great length. After listening patiently, the physician took a small phial, opened it, and held it under the lord's nose. "Smell!" cried the doctor. "Well, you are cured."

Somewhat put out, his lordship asked, "How much do I owe?"

"A thousand francs," replied the doctor.

The patient immediately pulled out a bank note, and, holding it under the physician's nose, cried "Smell! Well, you are paid."

Former Secretary of Health, Education, and Welfare Anthony Celebrezze once asked an elderly woman what she thought of Medicare. "Oh, I like it very much," she responded eagerly. "I took it for a month and lost ten pounds."

A man was complaining vociferously to his friend about his rheumatism. "There's no excuse for your being afflicted," said the friend. "I used to have rheumatism myself. When it would act up, I would go home and have my wife throw her arms around my neck and give me a massage treatment. It worked every time," he went on. "You ought to try it."

"I sure will," replied the man. "What time does your wife get home?"

Nothing soothes me more after a long and maddening course of pianoforte recital than to sit and have my teeth drilled.

—George Bernard Shaw

A waiter in a large metropolitan restaurant was suddenly stricken and rushed to the hospital's emergency room. Lying on the operating table in great pain while awaiting attention, he saw an intern passing by.

"Doc," he said desperately, "I'm sick. Can't you do something?"

"Sorry," replied the intern. "This isn't my table."

About to have her baby, a woman was rushed to the hospital. However, she was just a bit late, and had the child on the hospital lawn. When her husband asked for the bill a few days later, he noticed that the first charge read "Delivery Room fee—$25."

The husband protested that the baby had been born not in the delivery room but on the lawn. The deadpan clerk simply crossed out "Delivery Room fee—$25" and wrote in its place "Greens fee—$25."

"Doc," said the old hillbilly, leading a gangling youth toward the town physician, "I want you to fix up my son-in-law. I shot him in the leg yesterday and lamed him up a mite."

"Shame on you," the doctor scolded, "shooting your own son-in-law."

"Waal, Doc," countered the hillbilly, "he warn't my son-in-law when I shot him."

My diseases are an asthma and a dropsy and, what is less curable, seventy-five.

—Samuel Johnson

During World War II an army doctor stationed at a remote dispensary in the South Pacific was uncertain about the method of treatment for one of his patients. Since his own facilities were inadequate, he radioed a query to the nearest base hospital: "Have a case of beriberi. What shall I do?"

Some wag at the hospital radioed back, "Give it to the Marines—they'll drink anything."

Suffering from a serious liver disease, Tom Smith consulted an eminent surgeon for an operation. Soon after he had recovered from the anesthetic, the doctor visited him in the hospital room for a checkup. "How does your side feel?" he queried gaily.

"Oh, my side feels fine," croaked Smith, "but I have this awful pain in my throat. What's wrong with it, Doc?"

"Well," began the surgeon hesitantly, "I guess I'd better tell you. You see, I performed the operation in that big amphitheater. It's quite a tense atmosphere in there, with all those people watching your every move.

"Yours happens to have been a very unusual case—some doctors might never see one like it for a lifetime. The operation itself lasted nearly two hours. But I was lucky, my hands were steady as rocks, and I achieved perfect results.

"When it was all over, I stood back from the operating table, and the whole amphitheater erupted into applause. The medical students gave me a standing ovation. In fact, Smith, the acclaim was so loud and prolonged that . . . well . . . I took out your tonsils for an encore."

The story is told among doctors that there was once a man who was so deeply averse to paying doctor bills that he finally purchased a book on medicine and, with the knowledge contained therein, successfully treated himself for a number of years. He eventually died of a misprint.

At a recent AMA dinner in San Francisco, one Dr. Alton Ochsner turned to a colleague and asked, "Do you know the first oral contraceptive?"

"No," his colleague responded.

"Right!" rejoined Dr. Ochsner.

Reports have it that a researcher is attempting to develop a medicated gas which will deodorize and sanitize the cages of animals. The process will be known as Medical Air for the Cagèd.

"Oh, dear," sighed the sweet young thing. "Will the scar show, Doctor?"

"That, young lady," replied the physician gravely, "is entirely up to you.

A cub reporter, interviewing an old-timer who had reached his 99th birthday, told him, "I certainly hope I can come next year and see you reach 100."

"Can't think why not," responded the old gentleman. "You look healthy enough to me."

During one medical-school class on abdominal surgery, the professor had occasion to ask a young female student, "Have you read Hare on the abdomen?"

"Why, Doctor," blushed the girl, "I'm a brunette."

A middle-aged man was complaining to his doctor that he was not feeling quite up to snuff.

"Do you drink much?" asked the physician.

"No, not at all," replied the patient.

"Do you smoke?"

"No."

"Overeat?"

"Why, no. As a matter of fact, I'm a light eater, and I don't touch sweets or starchy foods."

"Well," pursued the doctor, "how about the other indulgences—like gambling, women, or the like?"

"Oh my heavens, no," said the man, genuinely shocked.

"You certainly are a most unusual man," said the physician admiringly. "What seems to be troubling you?"

"It's just my back," responded the patient. "I have this sharp pain from time to time across my shoulder blades."

"Well," smiled the doctor, "that's only to be expected. You're not wearing your wings properly."

God heals, the doctor takes the fee.
—Benjamin Franklin
Poor Richard's Almanac